Anonymous

Gate of Heaven or, Way of the Child of Mary

A manual of prayers and instructions, compiled from approved sources for the use

of young persons

Anonymous

Gate of Heaven or, Way of the Child of Mary
A manual of prayers and instructions, compiled from approved sources for the use of young persons

ISBN/EAN: 9783337302931

Printed in Europe, USA, Canada, Australia, Japan

Cover: Foto ©Lupo / pixelio.de

More available books at **www.hansebooks.com**

GATE OF HEAVEN

OR,

WAY OF THE CHILD OF MARY.

A MANUAL OF

PRAYERS AND INSTRUCTIONS,

COMPILED FROM APPROVED SOURCES

FOR THE USE OF YOUNG PERSONS.

ILLUSTRATED WITH FORTY PLATES.

A NEW AN REVISED EDITION.

TURNHOUT.

BREPOLS & DIERCKX, SON.

APPROVED.

CONTENTS.

	PAGE
Table of Movable Feasts	11
Conduct of Children in Churches	13
Feasts and Fasts throughout the year	19
The Manner of Lay Persons Baptizing an Infant, in Danger of Death	22
A Brief Statement of Christian Doctrine	22
INSTRUCTIONS AND DEVOTIONS FOR MORNING	30
Our Father, Hail Mary	35
Apostles' Creed and Confiteor	36
Acts of Faith, Hope, Charity and Contrition	87
Prayers to the Blessed Virgin, Angel Guardian and Patron Saint	39
LITANY OF THE HOLY NAME OF JESUS	40
Salve Regina	44
Memorare	45
Prayers on Going into Church	46
Taking Holy Water	46
Grace before and after meat	46
The Angelus	46
Evening Prayers	48
LITANY OF THE BLESSED VIRGIN (Latin and Englisch	52
A PRAYER FOR RELATIONS AND FRIENDS	62
Scholar's	62
To the infant Jesus	62

CONTENTS.

	PAGE
Prayer to Holy Mary	64
An Offering of oneself to the Blessed Virgin	65
Ejaculations	66
Christian Duties	67
Prayers for the Dead, (*De Profundis*)	69
Prayers on taking Holy Water	71
INSTRUCTIONS FOR HEARING MASS	72
Devotions for Holy Mass	74
Prayer when preparing for first Communion	165
INSTRUCTIONS FOR CONFESSIONS	168
Examinations of Conscience	168
Act of Contrition	173
Thanksgiving after Confession	174
A Prayer for renewing our Baptismal Vows	176
INSTRUCTIONS FOR COMMUNION	178
Prayers before Communion	179
Acts of Thanksgiving after Communion	183
Act of Offering after Communion	187
INSTRUCTIONS FOR CONFIRMATION	189
Prayer before Confirmation	190
Prayer to the Holy Ghost	192
Ceremony of Confirmation	193
Prayer after Confirmation	199
PIOUS PRACTICES IN HONOR OF THE SACRED HEART OF JESUS	202
Office of the Sodality of the Sacred Heart	205
Act of Atonement to the Sacred Heart of Jesus	226
Act of Consecration to the Adorable Heart of Jesus	227
ORIGIN AND END OF THE SODALITY TO THE B. V. M.	228
Advantages of the Sodality	230
General Rules of the Sodality	235
Little Office of the Immaculate Conception	239

CONTENTS.

	PAGE
Formula of admission to the Sodality	249
Prayer of S. Aloysius of Gonzaga to the B. Virgin	250
Prayer after Holy Communion	251

ASSOCIATION OF THE HOLY INFANCY 252

WARNING TO CHILDREN 259

ADVICE OF ST. PHILIP NERI TO HIS SPIRITUAL CHILDREN 262

LITANIES.
- Of the Holy Name of Jesus 40
- Of the Blesssed Virgin Mary 52
- Of the Saints 266
- Of the Sacred Heart of Jesus 277
- Of the Sacred Heart of Mary 280
- Of the Immaculate Conception 282
- Of the Children of Mary 285
- Of the Holy Angel Guardian 288
- Of St. Joseph 290
- Of St. Vincent of Paul 295
- Of St. Aloysius 296
- For Children 304

Seven Penitential Psalms 305

VESPERS 315
- Hymn, Lucis Creator optime 335

BENEDICTION OF THE MOST HOLY SACRAMENT. 348
- Hymn, O salutaris Hostia 348
- Hymn, Pange Lingua Gloriosi 349
- Veni Creator Spiritus, (*Withsun-tide*) . . 354
- Ave maris Stella 356
- St. Casimir to the Blessed Virgin, Mother of God: in six decades 358
- Adeste Fidelis, (for Christmas) 372
- Veni Sancte Spiritus 374
- Of the Blessed Sacrament 376

CONTENTS.

HYMNS.

	PAGE
Dolors of the Blessed Virgin Mary	380
For Trinity Sunday	384
Jesus, Redeemer of the World	386
For Christmas	386
For the Epiphany	387
Most holy Name of Jesus	388
For Lent	389
The Holy Cross, for Passion Tide	390
The Crucifixion	391
For Easter	392
Sacred Heart of Jesus	393
Feast of the Annunciation	394
For Ascension Day	395
For Advent	396
To St. Joseph	397
All Saints	397
To St. Michael	398
The Precious Blood	399
Guardian Angel—Morning and Evening	401
For Little children on the Infancy of Jesus	402
"Suffer Little Children to come unto Me."	404
Heavenly Home	405
St. Francis Xavier	406
Immaculate Conception	408
I am a faithful Catholic	411
Two Thousand Years Ago	412
Daily, Daily, Sing to Mary	414
Sweet Month of May	416
I am a Little Catholic	418
St. Patrick	419
All Praise to St. Patrick	420
The Month of Mary	422
God Bless Our Pope	423
Te Deum Laudamus	425
ASPERGES ME; or SPRINKLING OF HOLY WATER	429
Prayer for the Authorities	431
THE MANNER OF SERVING AT MASS	435

TABLE OF MOVABLE FEASTS.

Year of our Lord	Dominical Letter	Golden number.	The Epact.	Septuagesima Sunday	Ash Wednesday.	Easter Sunday.
1885	d	5	xiv	Feb. 1	Feb.18	April 5
1886	c	6	xxv	Feb.21	Mar.10	April 25
1887	b	7	vi	Feb. 6	Feb.23	April 10
1888	A g	8	xvii	Jan.29	Feb.15	April 1
1889	f	9	xxviii	Feb.17	Mar. 6	April 21
1890	e	10	ix	Feb. 2	Feb.19	April 6
1891	d	11	xx	Jan.25	Feb.11	Mar. 29
1892	c b	12	i	Feb 14	Mar.11	April 17
1893	A	13	xii	Jan.29	Feb.15	April 2
1894	g	14	xxiii	Jan.21	Feb. 7	Mar. 25
1895	f	15	iv	Feb.10	Feb.27	April 14
1896	e d	16	xv	Feb. 2	Feb.19	April 5
1897	c	17	xxvi	Feb.14	Mar. 3	April 18
1898	b	18	vii	Feb. 6	Feb.23	April 10
1899	A	19	xviii	Jan.29	Feb.15	April 2
1900	g	1	*	Feb.11	Feb.28	April 15
1901	f	2	xi	Feb. 3	Feb.20	April 7
1902	e	3	xxii	Jan.26	Feb.12	Mar. 30
1903	d	4	iii	Feb. 8	Feb.25	Avril 12
1904	c b	5	xiv	Jan.31	Feb.17	Avril 3
1905	A	6	xxv	Feb.19	Mar. 8	Avril 23
1906	g	7	xi	Feb.11	Feb.28	Avril 15
1907	f	8	xvii	Jan.27	Feb.13	Mars 31
1908	e d	9	xxviii	Feb.16	Mar. 4	Avril 19

TABLE OF THE MOVABLE FEASTS.

Year of our Lord	Ascencion-Day.	Whit-Sunday.	Corpus Christi.	Indiction.	Sundays after Pent	First Sunday of Advent
1885	May 14	May 24	June 4	13	26	Nov. 29
1886	June 3	June 13	June 24	14	23	Nov. 28
1887	May 19	May 29	June 9	15	26	Nov. 27
1888	May 10	May 20	May 31	1	27	Dec. 2
1889	May 30	June 9	June 20	2	24	Dec. 1
1890	May 15	May 25	June 5	3	26	Nov. 30
1891	May 7	May 17	May 28	4	27	Nov. 29
1892	May 26	June 5	June 16	5	24	Nov. 27
1893	May 11	May 21	June 1	6	27	Dec. 3
1894	May 3	May 13	May 24	7	28	Dec. 2
1895	May 23	June 2	June 13	8	25	Dec. 1
1896	May 14	May 24	June 4	9	26	Nov. 29
1897	May 27	June 6	June 17	10	24	Nov. 28
1898	May 19	May 29	June 9	11	25	Nov. 27
1899	May 11	May 21	June 1	12	27	Dec. 3
1900	May 24	June 3	June 14	13	25	Dec. 2
1901	May 16	May 26	June 6	14	26	Dec. 1
1902	May 8	May 18	May 29	15	27	Nov. 30
1903	May 21	May 31	June 11	1	25	Nov. 29
1904	May 12	May 22	June 2	2	26	Nov. 27
1905	June 1	June 11	June 22	3	24	Dec. 3
1906	May 24	June 3	June 14	4	25	Dec. 2
1907	May 9	May 19	May 30	5	27	Dec. 1
1908	May 28	June 7	June 18	6	24	Nov. 29

CONDUCT OF CHILDREN IN CHURCHES.

If Christians would only reflect on the sanctity of our temples, they would certainly treat them with greater respect. They are holy, because God fills them with his presence, as he himself tels us by the prophet Aggeus : *I will fill that house with my glory, I will establish peace in that place.* They are holy because they contain the source of all grace, because in them is dispensed the word of God, and finally, because the Lord has promised to hear with favour all those who go there to solicit his mercy; *Mine eyes are open, and mine ears attentive to the prayer of him who cometh to pray in my temple.*

Jesus-Christ declares in the Gospel that his house is a house of prayer. It is not only the material edifice that we should respect : if the Jews were penetrated with the most profound respect on entering their temple, (a noble but imperfect image of ours) can we, who possess the reality of their figures, even Christ himself present on our altars, can we fal in respect or veneration without offending our good Saviour. If our faith were not so enfeebled as it is, would it be necessary to give children lessons of modesty, and of proper behaviour in the house of God? Should not parents make it a duty to teach them, by their own example, how they ought to demean themselves while in that holy place? But as we see with sorrow that the greater number of fathers and mothers neglect a point so important, we consider it our duty to lay down here a few rules which children should be made to observe while in church.

1st. Children should never be taken to church in a dress which would not be thought good enough for appearing before company.

2d. They sould be made to understand that the Lord penetrates the mind and heart, and desires that we should never enter his holy temple without being penetrated with the most profound respect; they sould be also taught to purify themselves from every fault that might render them unworthy of appearing in the presence of the Most High; to take the holy water with reverence, not plunging in the hand, but merely dipping the end of a finger; let them not throw it on the ground, nor sprinkle it on their own face, or that of another. They should be taught to enter into the spirit which animated David when he said, *Wash me yet more from mine iniquities, and purify me of my sins.*

3d. Children should not be permitted to ask any questions while in church, unless it relates to the celebration of the divine service. They ought to kneel and make a short prayer, ten take their seat, if possible, where they can see the ceremonies, and hear distinctly the word of God.

4th. If they are obliged to pass before the altar whereon is the Blessed Sacrament, they ought to bow down, and bend their knee before it in passing; going in front of other altars, it suffices te bow the head. It is exceedingly improper to jostle any one, or push them aside, even if they be in the way; they should be mildly requested to move a little, so as to leave room to pass; but if the crowd be too great, one must wait patiently till they can make ther way through.

As son as children have reached their place, they sould not be allowed to run here and there, even to speak to an acquaintance.

5th. The minds of children being incapable

of that fixed attention which excludes distraction, a book must be placed in their hand, containing the service which is going on, so that they may be enabled to join the faithful in the psalms and hymns, or in prayer; their parents are supposed to have previously instructed them in the different exercises of devotion, for it is no time for doing so when they should be joining in prayer, and following the psalms and hymns.

They should be early accustomed to preserve a decent and respectful demeanour while in the church, neither turning, their head from one side to the other, nor gazing around; they should be occupied solely with what is passing at the altar.

6th. The mass is the most august act of religion, and with what respect we ought to assist at its celebration! At low mass children should not be allowed to sit Down, if they are at all able to remain on their knees : at grand mass it is usual to sit during the *Kyrie Eleison*, the *Gloria*, the *Epistle*, the *Gradual*, and so on till the commencement of the Canon, standing up, however during the *Gospel*; during the *Canon* all are to kneel, except in a case where one is unable to do so. In churches where there are organs, children are in the habit of making various motions, keeping time with the music, either with their feet, head, or hands; they must be taught that all such conduct is highly improper, and that the holy joy inspired by the psalms and hymns, and the sacred music, should never carry the Christian so far as to make him lose sight of the respect and reverence due to the presence of God. At other times children fall asleep; if it be from weariness, they must be gently awoke, but if they really cannot remain awake, they ought to be taken home.

At other times children eat in the church, and this is exceedingly indecent and irreverent. *Have ye not houses wherein to eat or drink,* says St. Paul, *or do ye despise the Church of God?*

7th. Children should be accustomed to listen attentively to the word of God, so that they may not give way to weariness or drowsiness during the sermon or lecture; let them be severely corrected on reaching home, if they have effected to cough without any real necessity, to spit or use their handkerchief with a noise, during the discourse, or to stand up on a seat to look around.

8th. They should be inspired with a great respect not only for the priests of the Lord, and for all the ceremonies established by the Church, but also for every thing connected with religion and divine worship.

9th. It is not right to quit the church before the priest who said the mass has returned to the sacristy; nor after vespers, until the service is entirely finished.

10th. It is allowable to sit during vespers, but one should incline their head as often as the *Gloria Patri* is sung; all should remain standing until the first psalm is commenced, and also during the *Magnificat*, the prayers, he *Nunc Dimittis*, and the anthem to the Blessed Virgin.

11th. In processions which are made outside the Church, children should avoid disturbing the order of the ranks, by going or coming to and fro, walking now behind, now before, and sometimes close beside the priests; as also by singing louder, quicker, or slower than the chanters. It is also extremely disrespectful to look around on such ocsasions, gazing up at the windows, calling out or speaking to any one, chatting, laughing, running, or any other such indecorous behaviour.

FEASTS AND FASTS.

HOLY DAYS ON WHICH THERE IS STRICT OBLIGATION TO HEAR MASS, AND REMAIN FROM SERVILE WORK.

ALL Sundays in the year.

The Feast of the Circumcision of our Lord, Jan. I.

The Epiphany, Jan. 6.

The Annunciation of the Blessed Virgin, March 25.

Ascension of our Lord.

Corpus Christi, or the Feast of the Blessed Sacrament.

Assumption of the B. V. Mary, August 15.

Feast of all Saints, November 1.

Feast of the Immaculate Conception, Dec. 8.

Nativity of our Lord Jesus Christ December 25.

FASTING DAYS ON ONE MEAL.

All days in Lent, except Sundays.

The Eve of Whitsuntide.

The Quarter-Tenses, or Ember-days, which occur in the four seasons of the year, viz: the Wednesdays, Fridays, and Saturdays — 1. Immediately after the first Sunday in Lent; 2. In Whitsun-week; 3. Immediately after the 14th of September; 4. Immediately after the third Sunday of Advent.

The Vigil of the Assumption of the Blessed Virgin Mary, and the Vigil of all Saints.

Every Friday in Advent, and Christmas-Eve.

N. B. When a fasting day falls upon a Sunday, the Fast is observed on the Saturday preceding that Sunday.

DAYS OF ABSTINENCE FROM FLESH MEAT.

All the Sundays in Lent, except when the use of meat is allowed by the Archbishop or Bishop of the Diocese.

FEASTS AND FASTS. 21

All Fridays and Saturdays, except those Saturdays which fall between the 25th of December and the 2d of February, inclusively.

If Christmas-day fall upon a Friday or Saturday, neither fast nor abstinence is oberved.*

SPECIAL SEASONS.

The solemnization of marriage is forbidden from the first Sunday of Advent until after Twelfth day; and from the beginning of Lent until Low-Sunday.

* The abstinence on Saturdays is dispenced with, for the faithful throughout the United States, from 1840, except when a fast falls on Saturday. Hence, the Saturdays of Lent and Quarter-Tenses, and Vigils falling on Saturday, are still days of *abstinence* from *flesh meat*.

The time appointed for complying with the Easter duty begins on the first Sunday of Lent, and terminates on Trinity Sunday.

THE MANNER OF LAY PERSONS BAPTIZING AN INFANT, IN CASE OF DANGER OF DEATH.

Take common water, pour it on the head or face of the child; and, while you are pouring it, say the following words:

« I baptize thee in the † name of the Father, and of the Son, and of the Holy Ghost. Amen. »

NOTE. *Any person, whether man, woman, or child, may baptize an infant, in case of danger of death.*

A BRIEF STATEMENT
Of Christian Doctrine.

THE TEN COMMANDMENTS OF GOD. — Exodus xx.

I. I AM the Lord thy God, who brought thee out of the land of Egypt, and out of the house of bondage. Thou shalt not have strange gods before me. Thou shalt not make to thyself a graven thing, nor the likeness of any thing that is in heaven above, or in the earth beneath, nor of those things that are in the waters under the earth. Thou shalt not adore them, nor serve them : I am the Lord thy God, mighty, jealous, visiting the iniquity of fathers upon their children, unto the third and fourth generation of those that hate me; and showing mercy unto thousands of those that love me, and keep my commandments.

2. Thou shalt not take the name of the Lord thy God in vain; for the Lord will not hold him guiltless that shall take the name of the Lord his God in vain.

3. Remember that thou keep holy the Sabbath-day. Six days shalt thou labour, and shalt do all thy works; but on the seventh day is the Sabbath of the Lord thy God : thou sahlt do no work on it,

thou, nor thy son, nor thy daughter, nor thy man-servant, nor thy maid-servant, nor thy beast, nor the stranger that is within thy gates. For in six days the made heaven and earth, and sea, and all things tat are in them, and rested on the seventh day; therefore the Lord blessed the seventh day, and sanctified it.

4. Honor thy father and mother, that thou mayest be long-lived upon the land which the Lord thy God will give thee.

5. Thou shalt not kill.

6. Thou shalt not commit adultery.

7. Thou shalt not steal.

8. Thou sh lt not bear false witness against thy neighbour.

9. Thou shalt not covet thy neighbour's wife.

10. Thou shalt not covet thy neighbour's house, nor his servant, nor his ox, nor his ass, nor any thing that is his.

THE SIX PRECEPTS OF THE CHURCH.

1. To hear Mass on Sundays, and all holidays of obligation.

2. To fast and abstain on the days commanded.

3. To confess our sins at least once a year.

4. To receive the blessed Eucharist at Easter.

5. To contribute to the support of our pastors.

6. Not to solemnise marriage at the forbidden times; nor to marry persons within the forbidden degrees of kindred, or otherwise prohibited by the Church: nor clandestinely.

SEVEN SACRAMENTS.

Baptism, Matt. xxviii. 19. — Confirmation, Acts viii. 17. — Eucharist, Matt. xvi. 26. — Penance, John xx. 23. — Extreme Unction, James v. 14. — Holy Ordres, Luke xxii, 19. — Matrimony, Matt. xix. 6.

THE THREE THEOLOGICAL VIRTUES.

Faith — Hope — and Charity.

THE FOUR CARDINAL VIRTUES.

Prudence — Justice — Fortitude — and Temperance.

THE SEVEN GIFTS OF THE HOLY GHOST.
Isa. xi. 2, 3.

Wisdom, Understanding, Council, Fortitude, Knowledge, Piety, and The fear of the Lord.

THE TWELVE FRUITS OF THE HOLY GHOST.

Charity, Joy, Peace, Patience, Longanimity, Goodness, Benignity, Mildness, Fidelity, Modesty, Continency, and Chastity.

THE SPIRITUAL WORKS OF MERCY.

To council the doubtful, To instruct ignorant, To admonish sinners, To comfort the afflicted, To forgive offences, To bear wrongs patiently, To pray for the living and the dead.

THE CORPORAL WORKS OF MERCY.

To feed the hungry, To give drink to the thirsty, To clothe the naked, To harbour the harbourless, To visit the sick, To visit the captive, and To bury the dead.

THE EIGHT BEATITUDES. — Matt. v.

1. Blessed are the poor in spirit; for theirs is the kingdom of heaven.
2. Blessed are the meek; for they shall possess the land.
3. Blessed are they that mourn; for they sall be comforted.
4. Blessed are they that hunger and thirster after justice; for they shall be filled.
5. Blessed are the merciful; for they shall obtain mercy.

6. Blessed are the clean of heart; for they shall see God.

7. Blessed are the peacemakers; for they shall be called the children of God.

8. Blessed are they that suffer persecution for justice' sake; for theirs is the kingdom of heaven.

THE SEVEN DEADLY SINS, AND THE OPPOSITE VIRTUES.

Pride, Covetousness, Lust, Anger, Gluttony, Envy and Sloth.

CONTRARY VIRTUES.

Humility, Liberality, Chastity, Meekness, Temperance, Brotherly love, and Diligence.

SINS AGAINST THE HOLY GHOST.

Presumption of God's mercy — Despair — Impugning the known truth — Envy at another's spiritual good — Obstinacy in sin — Final impenitence.

SINS CRYING TO HEAVEN FOR VENGEANCE.

Wilful Murder — The sin of Sodom — Oppresion of the poor — Defrauding labourers of their wages.

NINE WAYS OF BEING ACCESSORY TO ANOTHER'S SIN.

By counsel — By command — By consent — By provocation — By praise or flattery — By concealment — By partaking — By silence — By defence of the ill done.

THE EMINENT GOOD WORKS.

Alms-deeds, or works of mercy — Prayer — and Fasting.

THREE EVANGELICAL COUNSELS.

Voluntary poverty — Chastity — and Obedience.

THE FOUR LAST THINGS TO BE REMEMBERED.

Death — Judgment — Hell — and Heaven.

Guide to Devotion.

INSTRUCTIONS AND DEVOTIONS FOR MORNING AND EVENING.

As soon as you awake make the ✠ of the cross, saying:

Glory be to the Father, who hath created me.

Glory be to the Son, who hath redeemed me.

Glory be to the Holy Ghost, who hath Sanctified me.

Blessed be the holy and undivided Trinity, now and for ever. Amen.

On rising from your bed, say:

In the name of our Lord Jesus-Christ, I arise. May he bless, preserve, and govern, me, and bring me to everlasting life. Amen.

While you are dressing, occupy yourself with pious thoughts and meditations, on some point in the life or passion of your Saviour, on God's mercies, on your own sins, on the temptations of the world, on the shortness of life, on eternity, etc.; or say some psalm or hymn.

As soon as you are dressed, prepare to say your morning prayers. There is no duty of greater importance than this; none has greater influence upon our lives. According as it is well or ill performed will be the character of the day; and our life is made up of days. Before you begin your prayers, therefore, recollect yourself, and compose your mind. Think who you are, and what He is whom you are about to address; and endeavour to clothe yourself with those sentiments of humility, reverence, and awe, which become you on such an occasion, and at such a time. Then, kneeling down in the quietest and most retired spot you can find, if possible in some room or part of a room devoted to the purpose, begin your prayers.

MORNING PRAYERS.

Make the sign of te cross, saying.

In the name of the ✠ Father, and of the Son, and of the Holy Ghost. Amen.

Blessed be the holy and undivided Trinity, now and for ever. Amen.

Come, Holy Ghost, fill the hearts of thy faithful, and kindle in them the fire of thy love.

Send forth thy Spirit, and they shall be created, and thou shalt renew the face of the earth.

O God, who hast taught the hearts of the faithful by the light of thy Holy Spirit; grant us, in the same Spirit, to know what is right, and ever to rejoice in his consolation, through Jesus Christ our Lord. Amen.

Place yourself in the presence of God.

Most holy and adorable Trinity, one God in three persons, I believe that thou art here present; I adore thee with the deepest humility, and render to thee with my whole heart, the homage which is due to thy sovereign majesty.

Thank God, and offer yourself to Him.

My God, I most humbly thank thee for all the favours thou hast bestowed upon me up to the present moment. I give thee thanks from the bottom of my heart that thou hast created me after thine own image and likeness, that thou hast redeemed me by the precious blood of thy dear Son, and that thou hast preserved me and brought me safe to the beginning of another day. I offer to thee, O Lord, my whole being, and in particular all my thoughts, words, actions, and sufferings of this day, I consecrate them all to the glory of thy name, beseeching thee that through the infinite merits of Jesus Christ my Saviour they may all find acceptance in thy sight.

Resolve to avoid sin, and to practise holiness.

Adorable Jesus, my Saviour and Master, model of all perfection, I resolve and will endeavour this day to imitate thy example, to be like thee, mild, humble, chaste, zealous, charitable, and resigned. I will strive to avoid those sins which I have heretofore committed (*here you may name any besetting sin*), and which I sincerely desire to forsake.

Implore the necessary graces.

O my God, thou knowest my weakness, and that I am unable to do any thing good without thee; deny me not O God, the help of thy grace; give me strength to avoid everything evil which thou forbiddest, and to practise the good which thou hast commanded; and enable me to bear patiently the trials which it may please thee to send me.

PATER NOSTER.

Our Father, who art in heaven, hallowed be thy name : thy kingdom come : thy will be done on earth as it is in heaven. And forgive us our trespasses, as we forgive them that trespass against us. And lead us not into temptation; but deliver us from evil. Amen.

AVE MARIA.

Hail, Mary, full of grace : the Lord is with thee : blessed art thou among women, and blessed is the fruit of thy womb, Jesus. Holy Mary, Mother of God, pray for us sinners, now and at the hour of our death. Amen.

CREDO.

I believe in God, the Father Almighty, Creator of heaven and earth. And in Jesus Christ, his only Son, our Lord; who was conceived by the Holy Ghost, born of the Virgin Mary, suffered under Pontius Pilate, was crucified, dead, and buried : he descended into hell; the third day he rose again from the dead; he ascended into heaven, and sitteth at the right hand of God, the Father Almighty; from thence he shall come to judge the living and the dead. I believe in the Holy Ghost the holy Catholic Church, the communion of Saints, the forgiveness of sins, the resurrection of the body, and the life everlasting. Amen.

CONFITEOR.

I confess to Almighty God, to blessed Mary ever Virgin, to blessed Michael the Archangel, to blessed John the Baptist, to the holy Apostles Peter and Paul, and to all the Saints, that I have sinned exceedingly, in thouhgt, word, and deed, through my fault, through my fault, through my most grievous fault. Therefore I beseech the blessed Mary ever Virgin, blessed Michael the Archangel, blessed John the Baptist, the holy Apostles Peter and Paul, and all the Saints, to pray to the Lor d our God for me.

May Almighty God have mercy, on me, forgive me my sins, and bring me to everlasting life. Amen.

May the almighty and merciful Lord grant me ✠ pardon, absolution, and remission of all my sins. Amen.

An Act of Faith.

O my God, I firmly believe all that thou hast revealed, and which the holy Catholic Church proposes to me to be believed, because thou art truth itself, which can neither deceive nor be deccived. In this faith I desire to live and die.

An Act of Hope.

O my God, relying on thy gracious promises, I hope, by the merits of Jesus Christ, for the pardon of my sins, grace to serve thee faithfully in this life by doing the good works which thou hast commanded, and eternal happiness in the world to come, trough Jesus-Christ our lord.

An Act of Love.

O my God, I love thee with my whole heart, and above all things, because thou art infinitely good in thyself and infinitely to be loved ; and for the love of thee I love my neighbour as myself; for the love of thee I forgive all who have injured me, and ask pardon of all whom I have injured.

An Act of Contrition.

O my God, I repent with my whole heart of having offended thee ; I detest my sins for the love of thee; I firmly resolve never to offend thee again, and by the help of thy grace to avoid every occasion of sin.

O HOLIEST Virgin, Mother of my God, and my especial Patroness! show thyself my mother, and take me under thy protection this day.

Angel of God, who art my guardian, enlighten, guard, direct, and govern me, who have been committed to thee by the supernal clemency. Amen.

And ye, O holy saints (NN.), my chosen and beloved patrons, intercede for me to God, that, by the guidance of his grace, I may love and praise him here; and hereafter, with you, behold his face for all eternity. Amen.

May our Lord bless us, and preserve us from all evil, and bring us to life everlasting; and may the souls of the faithful departed, through the mercy of God, rest in peace. Amen.

MORNING PRAYERS.

LITANY OF
THE HOLY NAME OF JESUS.

LORD have mercy upon us.
Lord have mercy upon us.
Christ have mercy upon us.
Christ have mercy upon us.
Lord have mercy upon us.
Lord have mercy upon us.
Christ hear us.
Christ graciously hear us.
God the Father of heaven,
God the Son, Redeemer of the world,
God the Holy Ghost,
Holy Trinity, one God,
Jesus, Son of the living God,
Jesus, Splendour of the Father,
Jesus, Brightness of eternal Light,
Jesus, King of glory,
Jesus, the Sun of justice,
Jesus, Son of the Virgin Mary,
Jesus, most admirable,

Have mercy upon us.

Jesus, the mighty God,
Jesus, the Father of the world to come,
Jesus, the Angel of great counsel,
Jesus, most powerful,
Jesus, most patient,
Jesus, most obedient,
Jesus, meek and humble of heart,
Jesus, Lover of Chastity,
Jesus, our Beloved,
Jesus, the God of peace,
Jesus, the Author of life,
Jesus, the Example of all virtues,
Jesus, the zealous Lover of souls,
Jesus, our God,
Jesus, our Refuge,
Jesus, the Father of the poor,
Jesus, the Treasurer of the faithful,
Jesus, the Good Shepherd,
Jesus, the true Light,
Jesus, the Eternal Wisdom,
Jesus, infinite Goodness,
Jesus, our Way and our Life,

Have mercy upon us.

Jesus, the Joy of Angels,
Jesus, the Joy of Angels,
Jesus, the Master of the Apostles,
Jesus, the Teacher of the Evange-
   lists,
Jesus, the Strength of Martyrs,
Jesus, the Light of Confessors,
Jesus, the Purity of Virgins,
Jesut, the Crown of all Saints,
Be merciful,
Spare us, O Jesus.
Be merciful.
Graciously hear us, O Jesus.
From all sin,
From thy wrath,
From the snares of the devil,
From the spirit of fornication,
From everlasting death,
From neglect of thy inspirations,
Through the mystery of thy holy
   Incarnation,
Through thy Nativity,
Through thy Infancy,
Through thy most divine Life,

Have mercy upon us.

Lord Jesus deliver us.

Through thy Labours,
Through thine Agony and Passion,
Through thy Cross and Dereliction,
Through thy Weariness and Faintness,
Through thy Death and Burial,
Through thy Resurrection,
Through thine Ascension,
Through thy Joys,
Through thy glory,

Lord Jesus, deliver us.

Lamb of God, who takest away the sins of the world.
Spare us, O Jesus.
Lamb of God, who takest away the sins of the world,
Graciously hear us, O Jesus.
Lamb of God, who takest away the sins of the world,
Have mercy on us, O Jesus.
Jesus, hear us.
Jesus, graciously hear us.

O Lord Jesus Christ, who hast said : « Ask, and ye shall receive; seek, and ye shall find; knock, and it shall be opened unto you; » grant, we beseech thee, to us who ask the gift of thy divine love, that we may love thee with our whole hart, in word and work, and never cease from showing forth thy praise.

O God, who hast appointed thine only-begotten Son the Saviour of mankind, and hast commanded that he sould be called Jesus; mercifully grant, that we may enjoy in heaven the blessed vision of Him, whose holy Name we venerate upon earth. Through the name our Lord. Amen.

SALVE REGINA.

Hail, holy Queen, Mother of Mercy;

Our life, our sweetness, and our hope, all hail.

To thee we cry, poor banished sons of Eve;

To thee we sigh, weeping and mourning in this vale of tears.

Therefore, O our Advocate,

MORNING PRAYERS. 45

Turn thou on us those merciful eyes of thine;
And after this our exile, show us
The blessed fruit of thy womb, Jesus.
O merciful, O kind, O sweet Virgin Mary.
V. Pray for us, O holy Mother of God.
R. That we may be made worthy of the promises of Christ.

MEMORARE.

Remember, O most gracious Virgin Mary, that never was it known, tat any one who fled to thy protection, implored thy help, and sought thy intercession, was left unaided. Inspired with this confidence, I fly unto thee, O Virgin of virgins, my Mother. To thee I come; before thee I stand, sinful and sorrowful.* O Mother of the Word Incarnate, despice not my petitions, but in thy mercy hear and answer me. Amen.

* Here you may make your request.

MORNING PRAYERS.

ON GOING INTO CHURCH.

O Lord, in the multitude of thy mercies, I will enter into thy house, and praise thy holy name.

AT TAKING HOLY WATER.

Purify my heart and lips, O Lord, that I may be worthy to offer up my prayers to thee.

GRACE BEFORE MEAT.

V. Bless us, O Lord, and these thy gifts, which of thy bounty we are about to receive; through Christ our Lord.

R. Amen.

GAACE AFTER MEAT.

We give thee thanks, Almighty God, for all thy benefits; who livest and reignest, world without end. Amem.

Vouchsafe, O Lord, to render to all who do us good, for thy name's sake, life everlasting. *R.* Amen.

THE ANGELUS.

To be said Morning, Noon, and Night.

I. The Angel of the Lord announced

unto Mary. *R.* And she conceived of the Holy Ghost.

Hail, Mary, full of grace, the Lord is with thee; blessed art thou among women, and blessed is the fruit of thy womb, Jesus. Holy Mary, mother of God, pray for us sinners, now and at the hour of our death. Amen.

II. Behold the handmaid of the Lord.

B. Be it done unto me according to thy word.

Hail, Mary, &c.

III. And the word was made flesh.

R. And dwelt among us.

Hail, Mary, &c.

Pour forth, we beseech thee, O Lord, thy grace into our hearts; that we, to whom the incarnation of Christ thy Son was made known by the message of an angel, may by his passion and cross, be brought to the glory of his resurrection; through the same Christ our Lord. Amen.

Evening Prayers.

Make the sign of the cross, saying:

In the name of the ✠ Father, and of the Son, and of the Holy Ghost. Amen.

Blessed be the holy and undivided Trinity, now and for ever. Amen.

Come, Holy Ghost, fill the hearts of thy faithful, and kindle in them the fire of thy love.

Send forth thy Spirit, and they shall be created, and thou shalt renew the face of the earth.

Our Father. Hail Mary. I believe, (*as before*, p. 35.)

1. *Place yourself in the presence of God.*

O Almighty and eternal God, whose majesty filleth heaven and earth, I firmly believe that thou art here present; that thy all-seeing eye is upon me; that thou knowest all things, and art acquainted with the most secret thoughts of my heart. I desire to bow down all the powers of my soul to adore thee; I desire to join my voice with all thy blessed angels and saints, to praise thee and glorify thee now and for ever.

2. *Give Thanks.*

I most heartily thank thee, O Lord, for all thy mercies and blessings bestowed upon me and upon thy wole Church; and particularly for those I have received from thee this day, in watching over me, and preserving me from the many evils and dangers to which I am exposed. *(Here pause and medidate on God's mercies.)* Oh, let me never more be ungrateful unto thee, my God, who art so good and gracious unto me.

3. *Ask for light to discover your sins.*

And now, dear Lord, add this one blessing to the rest; that I may clearly discover the sins which I have committed this day, by thought, word, and deed, or by any omission of any part of my duty to thee, to my neighbour, or to myself, that no part of my guilt may be hidden from my own eyes, but that I may see my sins, and may hate them as I ought.

4. *Daily examination.*

Examine your consicence, and consider where and in what company you have been this day. Call to mind the sins committed against God, your neighbour, or yourself.

Have I been disrespectful at Mass and during prayers, by thinking of something else, or looking about? Have I said my prayers in a hurry, or without attention? Have I spoken of sacred things with want of respect? Have I not been sorry for my sins, or tried to correct my bad habits?

Have I been disobedient to my parents, or my teachers, or ill-humoured against them? or have I amswered with disrespect, when they have found fault with me, or not listened properly to their instructions and advice?

EVENING PRAYERS. 51

Have I been angry and quarelled with my brothers, sisters, or companions, and wished to revenge, myself by striking them, or any other ill-natured action? Have I not helped them when they wanted my assistance, or not borne with their defects? Have I laughed at my neighbour's faults? Have I been proud or vain?

Have I been idle or inattentive at my studies? Have I told untruths to excuse myself? Have I said or done any thing contrary to modesty, or have I been greedy? Have I been impatient and sulky, and not taken any pains to get rid of my bad habits?

5. *An Act of Contrition.*

O heavenly Fater! I acknowledge and confess, and am heartily sorry for, all the sins of my past life, and of this day in particular. I grieve from the bottom of my heart that I have been so ungrateful to thee for thy benefits, and have so often offended thee, my God and my chief good. Spare me, I beseech thee, by the death and love of Jesus Christ thy Son; and mercifully forgive me whatsoever sins I have this day, or heretofore, committed against thee, my neighbour, or myself.

6. *A Resolution of Amendment.*

O Almighty God! I firmly resolve, here in thy presence, and before the whole company of heaven, to live henceforth in more strict obedience to thy commandments. I resolve to keep a closer watch over myself; to correct my evil habits; to attend more diligently to my duties; to avoid more carrefully all sin, and whatever may lead to it.

LITANY OF
The Blessed Virgin Mary.

Ant. Sub tuum præsidium confugimus, sancta Dei Genitrix, nostras deprecationes ne des-

Ant. We fly to thy patronage, O holy Mother of God despise not our petitions in our neces-

EVENING PRAYERS.

picias in necessitatibus nostris; sed a periculis cunctis libera nos semper, Virgo gloriosa et benedicta.

Kyrie eleison.
Kyrie eleison.
Christe eleison.
Christe eleison.
Kyrie eleison.
Kyrie eleison.
Christe audi nos.
Christe exaudi nos.

Pater de cœlis Deus,
Fili Redemptor mundi Deus,

Spiritus Sancte Deus,
Sancta Trinitas, unus Deus,

Miserere nobis.

sities; but deliver us always from all dangers, O glorious and blessed Virgin.

Lord have mercy.
Lord have mercy.
Christ have mercy.
Christ have mercy.
Lord have mercy.
Lord have mercy.
Christ hear us.
Christ graciously hear us.

God the Father of heaven,
God the Son, Redeemer of the world,
God the Holy Ghost,
Holy Trinity, one God,

Have mercy on us.

EVENING PRAYERS.

Sancta Maria,	Holy Mary,
Sancta Dei Genitrix,	Holy Mother of God,
Sancta Virgo virginum,	Holy Virgin of virgins,
Mater Christi,	Mother of Christ,
Mater divinæ gratiæ,	Mother of divine grace,
Mater purissima,	Mother most pure,
Mater castissima,	Mother most chaste,
Mater inviolata,	Mother inviolate,
Mater intemerata,	Mother undefiled,
Mater amabilis,	Mother most amiable,
Mater admirabilis,	Mother most admirable,
Mater Creatoris,	Mother of our Creator,
Mater Salvatoris,	Mother of our Saviour,
Virgo prudentissima,	Virgin most prudent,
Virgo veneran-	Virgin most

Ora pro nobis. — *Pray for us.*

EVENING PRAYERS.

randa,	venerable,
Virgo prædicanda,	Virgin most renowned,
Virgo potens,	Virgin most powerful,
Virgo clemens,	Virgin most merciful,
Virgo fidelis,	Virgin most faithful,
Speculum justitiæ,	Mirror of justice,
Sedes sapientiæ,	Seat of wisdom,
Causa nostræ lætitiæ,	Cause of our joy,
Vas spirituale,	Spiritual Vessel,
Vas honorabile,	Vessel of honor,
Vas insigne devotionis,	Singular Vessel of devotion,
Rosa mystica,	Mystical Rose,
Turris Davidica,	Tower of David,
Turris eburnea,	Tower of ivory,
Domus aurea,	House of gold,
Fœderis arca,	Ark of the covenant,
Janua cœli,	Gate of heaven,
Stella matutina,	Morning star,
Salus infirmorum,	Health of the sick,

Ora pro nobis. — *Pray for us.*

Refugium peccatorum,	Refuge of sinners,
Consolatrix afflictorum,	Comforter of the afflicted,
Auxilium Christianarum,	Help of Christians,
Regina Angelorum,	Queen of Angels,
Regina Patriarcharum,	Queen of Patriarchs,
Regina Prophetarum,	Queen of Prophets,
Regina Apostolorum,	Queen of Apostles,
Regina Martyrum,	Queen of Martyrs,
Regina Confessorum,	Queen of Confessors,
Regina Virginum,	Queen of Virgins,
Regina Sanctorum omnium,	Queen of all Saints,
Regina sine labe originali concepta,	Queen conceived without original sin,

Ora pro nobis. — *Pray for us.*

Agnus Dei, qui Lamb of God,

EVENING PRAYERS.

tollis peccata mundi,
 Parce nobis, Domine.
 Agnus Dei, qui tollis peccata mundi,
 Exaudi nos, Domine.
 Agnus Dei, qui tollis peccata mundi,
 Miserere nobis.
 Christe audi nos.
 Christe exaudi nos.
 Ant. Sub tuum præsidium, &c.
 V. Ora pro nobis, sancta Dei Genitrix.
 R. Ut digni efficiamur promissionibus Christi.
 Gratiam tuam, quæsumus, Domine, mentibus nostris in-

who takest away the sins of the world,
 Spare us, O Lord.
 Lamb of God, who takest away the sins of the world,
 Graciously hear us, O Lord.
 Lamb of God, who takest away the sins of the world,
 Have mercy on us.
 Christ hear us.
 Christ graciously hear us.
 Ant. We fly to thy patronage, &c.
 V. Pray for us, O holy Mother of God.
 R. That we may be made worthy of the promises of Christ.
 Pour forth, we beseech thee, O Lord, thy grace in-

funde: ut qui Angelo nuntiante, Christi Filii tui Incarnationem cognovimus, per Passionem ✠ ejus et Crucem ad Resurrectionis gloriam perducamur. Per eumdem Christum Dominum nostrum.

R. Amen.
V. Divinum auxilium maneat semper nobiscum.
R. Amen.

to our hearts; that we, to whom the Incarnation of Christ thy Son was made known by the message of an Angel, may by his Passion ✠ and Cross, be brought to the glory of his Resurrection. Through the same Christ our Lourd.

R. Amen.
V. May the divine assistance remain always with us.
R. Amen.

O my good angel, whom God has appointed to be my guardian, enlighten and protect me, direct and govern me this night. Amen.

O Lord, help us with thy grace when we are awake, and defend us by thy power while we are asleep; that whether we wake or sleep, the peace of our

Lord Jesus Christ may be with us.

Visit we beseech thee, O Lord, this habitation, and drive far from it all snares of the enemy. Let thy holy angels dwell therein to preserve us in peace; and let thy blessing be always upon us, through Christ our Lord. — Amen.

May the Almighty God be our guardian and our comforter; may he keep far from us bad dreams and vain imaginations, and preserve us pure in body and soul.

We fly to thy refuge, O holy Mary, and we implore thy aid. Turn thine eyes of compassion upon us, thy children, and protect us this night. Be to us always our most loving mother, and pour down upon us thy maternal benediction, O blessed, O sweetest Mary!

O you, my holy patrons, and all ye saints of God, pray for us, and obtain for us a quiet night and a happy death.

Bless, O Lord, the repose I am about

to take, that, my bodily strength being renewed, I may be the better enabled to serve thee.

And may the souls of the faithful departed through the mercy of God, rest in peace.

At our Evening Devotions.

Let us call to mind that death may surprise us this very night, and that the torments of hell are infinite and eternal. Let us endeavour so to lie down, so to take our rest, and so to rise, with the grace of God accompanyng us through life, that, when death shall come, we may awake to everlasting joy.

While you are undressing, be careful to observe the strictest modesty, and always remember your Guardian Angel, who never leaves you. Raise your thoughts to God, considering either the goodness of the Lord, the shortness of life, or the vanity of eartly things : or you may say to yourselves : « Time passes very quickly, and I am always drawing nearer to the grave. O my God, what will become of me if I continue to live as if I was not born for heaven! Lord, enlighten my mind, give me strength to form generous resolutions, and enable me to save my soul. » Before going to sleep, do not forget to make these ejaculations :

« Jesus, Mary, and Joseph, I give yon my heart and my soul.

« Jesus, Mary and Joseph, assist me in my last agony.

« Jesus, Mary and Joseph, may I die in peace in your blessed arms. »

And then say, « Into thy hands, O Lord, I commend my spirit. » Endeavour, if you can, to fall asleep with these words on your lips. Many of the saints have ended their lives with this ejaculation. If you will imitate the saints, you will die like saints; it is God himself who gives us this advice : « This is the way, walk ye in it. » (Is. xxx. 21.)

ADITIONAL PRAYERS.

A prayer for Relations, Friends, etc.

VOUCHSAFE, O Lord, to grand grace, mercy, and life everlasting, to my parents, brothers and sisters, and all my relations; as also to my godfathers and godmothers, my friends, and every other person for whom I am bound to pray, or who in any way stand in need of my prayers. And may the souls of the faithful departed, through the mercy of God, rest in peace. Amen.

The Scholar's Prayer.

Grand me, I most humbly beseech thee, O Lord, the grace of respect and obedience to my spiritual director, my master, (*or* mistress), teachers, and those whom my parents or guardians have placed in authority over me. Grant me also, O Lord, a diligence in learning my lessons, and above all, a watchfulness to avoid the conversation and company of all persons who offend thee by their wicked words or actions. Through our Lord Jesus-Christ. Amen.

To Jesus as an Infant.

I give thee thanks, most loving Jesus, because thou didst choose to veil the glories of thy divinity, and for our sake to become a little child, to be born in a poor etable of a poor mother, to be wrapt in mean clothes, and to be laid in a manger. Grant, dearest Jesus, that I may be like thee, humble and poor in spirit; and as thou wast obedient to thy Mother, the holy Virgin Mary, and to thy foster-father, the blessed St. Joseph, so I may be ever obedient to my earthly parents and teachers, for thy sake, who art my heavenly father and shepherd; that as I grow in age and stature, I may also grow day by day in wisdom and piety; and as thou, O my Saviour, didst choose wile on earth to live in poverty, so I may ever be disposed to honour and love the poor, to treat them kindly, and tho share with them whatever I may have. Give me, O Jesus, a mild, humble, loving, and compassionate spirit toward all men, striving in all things to imitate thy most perfect example. Hear this my prayer, O most merciful Saviour, I humbly beseech thee. Amen.

Prayer to Holy Mary.

O most blessed Virgin Mary, Mother of my Saviour, and my Mother, I commend myself to thy gracious protection during this day (*or* night), and for the rest of my life, and especially at the hour of my death. Watch over me with thy merciful and loving eyes; and grant that by thy holy intercession I may be preserved from all the snares and temptations to which my tender age is exposed, and may grow up in the exercice of all those graces which thou lovest, and in the fear and love of thy Son Jesus, so that I may one day be admitted to thy blessed society, and to the company of saints and angels in heaven, there to enjoy the presence of my God and Saviour for ever. Amen.

An offering of Oneself to the Blessed Virgin.

Most holy Virgin Mary, Mother of God, I, (—), desire to choose thee this day in presence of my angel guardian, and of all the heavenly court, for my special patroness, my advocate and my mother; I firmly resolve to love and serve thee, and to do all I can to induce others to love and serve thee also. I beseech thee, O my good and amiable mother, by the blood of thy Son shed for me, vouchsafe to receive me as thy child and thy perpetual servant : assist me in all my thoughts, my words, and my actions, at all moments of my life, so that all my deeds and al my thoughts, may be directed to the praise and glory of God; grant, by thy powerful intercession, that, having spent a holy life here on earth, I may be preserved from the dangers of eternal death, and may be conducted in safety to everlasting bliss. Amen.

Ejaculations.

O my God, teach me to love thee.

O my God, teach me to pray.

O my God, keep me from sin.

O my God, what wouldst thou have me do?

Lord, teach me wisdom.

My God, I love thee, and I love thee with all my heart.

Holy Mary, Mother of God, be a mother to me.

Mother of Christ, y take you for my mother.

Mother of divine grace, make me your child.

During the course of the day make these short ejaculations, and especially when tempted. Do you wish not to sin ? Prepare yourselves for temptations, watch, fly, pray. Watch over your mind, over your heart, over your senses ; sed a guard upon your eyes and upon your ears, which are as the doors through which sin enters the soul. Fly the occasions of sin, bad companions, and the reading of bad books ; never expose yourselves willingly to temptation. Always remember the presence of God, and thus you will be in a condition to conquer, and to merit the crown of glory. « Blessed is the man that endureth temptation, for, when he hath been proved he shall receive the crown of life. »

Christian Duties.

Remember, Christian soul, that thou hast this day, and every day of thy life,
God to glorify,
Jesus to imitate,

The angels and saints to invoke,
A soul to save,
A body to mortify,
Sins to expiate,
Virtues to acquire,
Hell to avoid,
Heaven to gain,
Eternity to prepare for,
Time to profit of,
Neighbours to edify,
The world to despise,
Devils to combat,
Passions to subdue,
Death perhaps to suffer,
And judgment to undergo.

Thou shalt love the Lord thy God with thy whole heart, and with thy whole soul, and with thy whole mind. This is the greatest and first commandment: and the second is like to this. — Thou shalt love thy neighbour as thyself. On these two commandments dependeth the whole law and the prophete. *S. Matt* xxii.

What it doth profit a man if he gain

ADDITIONAL PRAYERS. 69

the whole world and lose his own soul! *St. Matt.* xvi. 26.

PRAYERS FOR THE DEAD.

Ps. cxxix. *De Profundis.*

1. Out of the depths have I cried unto thee, O Lord: Lord, hear my voice.
2. Oh, let thine ears consider well: the voice of my supplication.
3. If thou, O Lord, shalt mark iniquities: Lord who shal abide it?
4. For with thee there is propitiation: and because of thy law I have waited for thee, O Lord.
5. My soul hath waited on his word: my soul hath hoped in the Lord.
6. From the morning watch even until night: let Israel hope in the Lord.
7. For with the Lord there is mercy: and with him plenteous redemption.
8. And he shall redeem Israel: from all his iniquities.

V. Eternal rest give unto them, O Lord.
R. And let perpetual ligt shine up on them.
V. May they rest in peace.
R. Amen.
V. From the gate of hell.
R. Deliver their souls, O Lord.
V. O Lord, hear my prayer,
R. And let my cry come unto thee.

Let us Pray.

O God, the Creator and Redeemer of all the faithful, give to the souls of thy servants departed the remission of all their sins : that, through pious supplications, they may obtain the pardon which they have always desired : who livest and reignest world without end. Amen.

V. Eternal rest give unto them, O Lord.
R. And let perpetual light shine upon them.

O God, bountiful in forgiving, and

lovingly desirous of man's salvation, we humbly beseech thy mercy in behalf of our friends, relations, and benefactors, who have passed from this world, that through the intercession of blessed Mary ever virgin and all the saints, thou wouldst permit them to come to the full participation of everlasting happiness. Through Christ our Lord. Amen.

On entering the Church, say:

I will enter Thy house, O Lord, and bless Thy Holy Name.

Taking holy water, make the sign of the † on yourself, and say:

Sprinkle me, O Lord, with hyssop, and I shall be cleansed: wash me, and I shall be whiter than snow.

INSTRUCTIONS FOR HEARING MASS.

Of all the duties proscribed by our holy Religion, the SACRIFICE of the MASS is that which is most pleasing to God, and most salutary to man. Here it is that Jesus-Christ renews the great mystery of our redemption : here doth he make himself our victim in a real, though unbloody sacrifice, and in person applieth to each of us the merits of that blood wich, hanging on the cross, he was pleased to shed for mankind. This should give us the most sublime idea of the Mass, and make us desire to hear it with the utmost reverence and devotion; for to assist at it irreverently, or without putting a proper restraint on our eyes and our whole exterior, is to dishonour religion, and renew, as far as in us lies, the insults he received on Mount Calvary. To avoid, then, so great an evil, let us always come to this august sacrifice with the most earnest devotion ; let us enter into the spirit of Christ; let us offer ourselves up with him, and as he does; let the church, as we enter it, strike us with awe; let our modesty and recollection be uninterrupted from the beginning to the end thereof; let our hearts, thoughts, and imaginations be, as it were, buried in God, and the interests of our souls.

Make a reverence before the Altar, before taking your place, and say:

I adore and bless Thee, o Lord Jesus Christ, Who, by Thy Cross, hast redeemed the world.

PRAYER BEFORE MASS BEGINS.

O Divine Jesus! Sacred Victim, offered to save mankind! Grant that I may assist at this holy Altar with Faith, with Hope, and with the most tender Love. Amen.

DEVOTIONS FOR MASS.

THE PRIEST GOES TO THE ALTAR.

In the name of the ✠ Father and of the Son, and of the Holy Ghost. Amen.

At the beginning of the Mass, the priest, at the foot of the altar, makes the sign of the cross, saying. « In the name of the Father, and of the Son, and of the Holy Ghost, Amen ; » and then recites with the clerk the 42d Psalm, « Judica me, Deus, &c. Judge me, O God. » *

---

* These explanations may be passed over by young children, but they will be found useful or others.

DEVOTIONS FOR MASS. 75.

The Priest goes to the Altar.

A PRAYER AT THE BEGINNING OF THE MASS.

I adore thee, O my God, and I firmly believe that the Mass, at which I am going to assist, is the sacrifice of the body and blood of thy Son Christ Jesus, my Saviour. Oh, grant that I may assist at it with the attention, reverence, and awe due to such a holy mystery; and grant that, by the merits of the Victim there offered for me, I myself may become an agreeable sacrifice tho the, who livest and reignest with the same Son and Holy Ghost, one God, world without end. Amen.

DEVOTIONS FOR MASS. 77

A prayer at the beginning of the Mass.

Then the priest, bowing down, says the *Confiteor*, « I confess to Almighty God, » &c., p. 36, by way of a general confession to God, to the whole court of heaven, and to all the faithful then present, of his sins and unworthiness; and to beg their prayers to God for him. And the clerk, in the name of the people, prays for the priest, that God would have mercy on him, and forgive him his sins, and bring him to everlasting life. Then, in the name of all there present, the clerk makes the like general confession to God, to the whole court of heaven, and to the priest, and begs his prayers.

And the priest prays to God tho show mercy to all his people, and to grant them pardon, absolution, and remission of all their sins. Which is done to the end that both priest and people may put themselves in a penitential spirit, in order to assist worthily at this divine sacrifice.

DEVOTIONS FOR MASS. 79

When the Priest, bowing down, says the
Confiteor.

A PRAYER AT THE CONFITEOR.

O my God, I bow down myself before thee, confessing that I have many ways offended thee in thought, word, and deed; and that I am not worthy of the many blessings thou bestowest upon me. Give me grace, O God, from this time te love the more, and to do always what is pleasing in thy sight. O blessed Virgin Mary, and all ye saints and angels, vouchsafe to intercede for me; and may the almighty and merciful Lord grant to us all pardon and peace. Amen.

DEVOTIONS FOR MASS. 81

When the Priest kisses the Altar.

After the Confiteor the priest goes up to the altar, saying:

« Take away from us, we beseech thee, O Lord, our iniquities, that we may be worthy to enter with pure minds into the holy of holies, through Christ our Lord. » Amen.

WHEN THE PRIEST KISSES THE ALTAR.

Say the same with him ; and when he kissed the altar, as a figure of Christ and the seat of the sacred mysteries, make an act of love of your divine Saviour, and embrace his feet with a humble and tender affection.

DEVOTIONS FOR MASS. 83

When the Priest goes to the Epistle
side of the Altar.

WHEN THE PRIEST GOES TO THE EPISTLE SIDE OR THE ALTAR.

When the priest is come up to the altar, he goes to the book, and there reads what is called the Introit, or Entrance, of the Mass, which is different every day and is generally a sentence taken out of the Scripture, with the first verse of one of the Psalms, and the « Glory be to the Father. » etc.

DEVOTIONS FOR MASS. 85

At the Introit.

AT THE INTROIT.

O my God, direct my steps, I beseech thee, in the way of thy commandments, and grant that nothing may ever separate me from thy love.

Blessed are they that are undefiled in the way; that walk in the law of the Lord.

Glory be to the Father. and to the Son, and to the Holy Ghost, as it was in the beginning, is now, and ever shall be, world without end. Amen.

AT THE KYRIE ELEISON.

The priest returns to the middle of the altar, and says alternately with the clerk the « Kyrie eleison, » or, « Lord have mercy on us, » which is said three times to God the Father; three times « Christe eleison, « or « Christ have mercy on us, « to God the Son; and three times again « Kyrie eleison, » to God the Holy Ghost.

After the Kyrie eleison, say the « Gloria in excelsis, » or « Glory to God on high, » &c., which is a beautiful hymn and prayer to God, the beginning of which was sung by the angels at the birth of Christ.

THE GLORIA IN EXCELSIS.

Glory to God on high, and on earth peace to men of good will. We praise thee, we bless thee, we adore thee, we glorify thee. We give thee thanks for

DEVOTIONS FOR MASS.

At the Kyrie eleison.

thy great glory. O Lord God, heavenly King, God the Father Almighty. O Lord Jesus Christ, the only-begotten Son, O Lord God, Lamb of God, Son of the Father, who takest away the sins of the world, have mercy on us : thou who takest away the sins of the world, hear our prayer : thou who sittest at the right hand of the Father, have mercy on us. For thou only art holy, thou alone art the Lord, thou only, o Jesus Christ, with the holy Ghost, art most high in the glory of God the Father. Amen.

AT THE DOMINUS VOBISCUM.

At the end of the « Gloria in excelsis » the priest kisses the altar, and, turning to the people, says, « Dominus vobiscum—The Lord be with you. » Answer, « Et cum spiritu tuo—And with thy spirit. » As often as this salutation is repeated, pray that our Lord may be always with you, with his ministers, and with his people, by directing and assisting all with his heavenly grace.

The priest then says, « Oremus—Let us pra , » and read the Collects of the day, concluding them with the usual termination, « Per Dominum nostrum, &c.—Through our Lord Jesus Christ, &c., » with which the Church commonly concludes all her prayers. Whilst the priest is reading the collects you may thus join with him :

DEVOTIONS FOR MASS. 91

At the Dominus vobiscum.

A PRAYER AT THE COLLECT.

O Almighty and eternal God, we humbly beseech thee mercifully to give ear to the prayers here offered thee by thy servant in the name of thy whole Church, and in behalf of us thy people. Accept them to the honor of thy name, and the good of our souls; and grant to us all mercy, grace, and salvation. Through our Lord Jesus Christ. Amen.

The collects being ended, the priest reads the epistle or lesson of the day. At the end of which the clerk answers, « Deo gratias—Thanks be to God, » namely, for the heavenly doctrine there delivered.

DEVOTIONS FOR MASS. 93

A prayer at the Epistle.

A PRAYER AT THE EPISTLE.

O my God, I thank thee that thou hast called me to the knowledge of thy holy law, while so many of my fellow creatures are left in darkness and ignorance. I desire to receive with all my heart thy divine commandments, and to hear with reverence the lessons which thou adressest to us by the mouth of thy prophets and apostles. Give me grace, O my God, not only to know thy will, but also to do it.

Then follow some sentences called the « Gradual, » which vary every day. »

AT MUNDA COR MEUM.

How wonderful, O Lord, is thy name in the whole earth. I will bless thee, O Lord, at all times; thy praise shall ever be in my mouth. Be thou my God and Protector for ever; I will put my whole trust in thee.

After this the book is removed to the other, or gospel side of the altar. The priest, before he reads the gospel, stands a while bowing down before the middle of the altar, begging of God, in secret, to cleanse his heart and his lips, that he may be worthy to declare those heavenly words. You may at the same time ask of God that he would open your ears and heart, that these divine lessons may sink deeply into your soul.

At munda cor meum.

At the beginning of the gospel the priest greets the people with the usual salutation, » Dominus vobiscum - The Lord be with you, » and then tells out of which of the evangelists the g spel is taken, saying « Sequentia S. Evangelii secundum &c.; that is, « What follows is of the holy Gospel according to St., &c., at which words both priest and people make the sign of the cross; first, upon their foreheads, to signify that they are not ashamed of the cross of Christ, and his doctrine; secondly, upon t eir mouths, to signify that they will ever profess it in their words; and thirdly. upon their breasts. to signify that they will always keep it in their hearts. The clerk answers, « Gloria tibi, Domine- Glory be to thee, O Lord. » At the gospel you stand up, to declare, by that posture, your readiness to do whatsoever your Saviour commands. If you have not the convenience of reading it, you may say as follows :

AT THE GOSPEL.

O Jesus, thou hast the words of eternal life; teach me, I beseech thee, what I must do to merit and obtain that life.

" If thou wilt enter into life, keep the commandments. —Thou shalt love the Lord thy God with thy whole heart, and with thy whole soul, and with thy whole mind, and with thy whole strength. Seek first the kingdom of God and his justice, and all other things shall be added unto you. — Be perfect, as your Father in heaven is perfect — Love your neighbor as yourself. — Love your

At the Gospel.

ennemies; do good to them that hate you, and pray for them that persecute you. — If any man will come after me, let him deny himself; let him take his cross and follow me. — Watch and pray, that you enter not into temptation. — Happy they who hear the word of God and keep it. »

O my Saviour, give me grace to lay to heart these and al thy holy precepts, and to practise them. What will it avail me to know the way of life, if I do not show forth in my conduct that I am thy disciple. O Jesus, help me to believe in thee, to love thee, and to imitate thee.

At the end of the gospel the clerk answers, « Laus tibi, Christe—Praise be to thee, O Christ. » And the priest kisses the book in reverence to those sacred words which he has been reading out of it. Then, upon all Sundays, and many other festival-days, standing in the middle of the altar, he recites the Nicene Creed, kneeling down at these words. « He was made man, » in reverence to the great mystery of our Lords incarnation.

I believe in one God, the Father Almighty, maker of heaven and earth, of all things visible and invisible. And in one Lord Jesus Christ, the only begotten Son of God, born of

the Father, before all ages;
God of God, Light of Light,
true God of true God; begotten, not made; consubstantial
to the Father; by whom all
things were made. Who for
us men, and for our salvation,
came down from heaven, and
was incarnate by the Holy
Ghost of the Virgin Mary, and
was made man. *(Here kneel.)*
He was crucified also for us,
suffered under Pontius Pilate,
and was buried. The third
day he rose again, according to
the Scriptures. He ascended
into heaven, and sitteth at the
right hand of the Father; and

he shall come again with glory to judge bot the living and the dead; of whose kingdom there shall be no end.

And I believe in the Holy Ghost, the Lord and Giver of life, who proceedeth from the Father and the Son; who, together with the Father and the Son, is adored and glorified; who spake by the prophets. And one holy catholic and apostolic Church. I confess one baptism for the remission of sins. And I looked for the resurrection of the dead, and the life of the world to come. Amen.

At the unveiling of the chalice.

AT THE UNVEILING OF THE CHALICE.

Then the priest turns to the people, and says, « Dominus vobiscum—The Lord be with you. » And having read in the book a verse or sentence of the Scripture, which is called the Offertory, and is every day different, he uncovers the chalice, and taking in his hand the paten, or little plate, offers up the bread to God; then going to the corner of the altar, he takes the wine and pours it into the chalice, and mingles with it a small quantity of water, in remembrance of the blood and water that issued out of the Saviour's side; after which he returns to the middle of the altar, and offers up te chalice. During the Offertory you may pray thus :

A PRAYER AT THE OFFERTORY.

Accept, O eternal Father, this offering which is here made to thee by thy minister, in the name of us all here present, and of thy whole Church. It is as yet only bread and wine, but, by a miracle of thy power and grace, will shortly become the body and blood of thy beloved Son. He is our High Priest, and he is our Victim. With him and through him we desire to approach to thee this day, and by his hands to offer thee this sacrifice, for thine own honour, praise, and glory; in thanksgiving for all thy bene-

A prayer at the offertory.

fits; in satisfaction for all our sins, and for obtaining conversion for all unbelievers, and mercy, grace, and salvation for all thy faithful. And with this offering of thine only-begotten Son, we offer ourselves to thee, begging that, through this sacrifice, we may be happily united to thee, and that nothing in life or death may ever separate us any more from thee. Through Jesus Christ our Lord. Amen.

AT THE COVERING OF THE CHALICE.

After the offering of the chalice, the priest bowing down, begs that this sacrifice, which he desires to offer with a contrite and humble heart, may find acceptance with God; and, blessing the bread and wine with the sign of te cross, he invokes the Author of all sanctity to sanctify the offering. You may join with him and say:

In a contrite heart and humble spirit may we be accepted by thee, O Lord; and let our sacrifice be pleasing in thy sight, O Lord God.

Come, O almighty and eternal God, the sanctifier, and bless this sacrifice prepared for thy holy name.

110   DEVOTIONS FOR MASS.

At the covering of the chalice.

DEVOTIONS FOR MASS. 111

At the end of the Offertory the priest goes to the corner of the altar and washes the tips of his fingers, to denote the cleanness and purity of soul with which we ought to approach to these divine mysteries, saying, « Lavabo, &c.—I will wash my hands among the innocent, and I wil compass thine altar, O Lord, » &c. (Ps. xxv. 6.)

A PRAYER AT THE LAVABO OR WASHING THE FINGERS.

O most pure and holy God, wash my soul, I beseech thee, from every stain, and grant that I may be worthy to assist with a clean heart at this most holy sacrifice.

A PRAYER WHEN THE PRIEST STANDS BOWING DOWN AT THE MIDDLE OF THE ALTAR.

O most holy and adorable Trinity, vouchsafe to receive this our sacrifice in remembrance of our Saviour's passion, resurrection, and glorious ascension: and let those saints, whose memory we celebrate on earth, remember us before thy throne

DEVOTIONS FOR MASS. 113

A prayer at the lavabo, or washing the fingers.

8

AT THE ORATE FRATRES.

in heaven, and obtain mercy for us, through the same Jesus Christ our Lord. Amen.

Then the priest, kissing the altar, turns to the people and says, « Orate, fratres, &c., that is, « Brethren, pray that my sacrifice and yours may be made acceptable to God the Father Almighty. » Pray, then, as he desires, and say:

Receive, O Lord, this sacrifice at the hands of thy minister, to the praise and glory of thine own name, for our benefit, and that of all thy holy Church.

Then the priest says, in a low voice, the prayers called the Secreta, which are different every day. During which, you may pray as follows:

DEVOTIONS FOR MASS. 115

At the Orate Fratres.

AT THE PREFACE.

Mercifully hear our prayers, O Lord, and graciously accept this oblation which we thy servants make to thee; and as we offer it to the honour of thy name, so may it be to us a means of obtaining thy grace here, and life everlasting hereafter. Through our Lord Jesus Christ. Amen.

The priest concludes the Secreta by saying aloud, « Per omnia sæcula sæculorum. » — « World without end. » *Answ..* « Amen. » *Priest.* « Dominus vobiscum—The Lord be with you. » *Ans.* « Et cum spiritu tuo—And with thy spirit. » *Priest.* « Sursum corda—Lift up your hearts. » *Ans.* « Habemus ad Dominum—We have lifted them up to the Lord. « *Priest.* « Gra-

DEVOTIONS FOR MASS. 117

At the Preface.

tias agamus Domino Deo nostro—
Let us give thanks to the Lord our
God. » *Ans.* « Dignum et justum est
—It is meet and just. »
Then the priest recites the Preface (so
called because it serves as introduction to the Canon of the Mass);
in which unite your adorations with
those which the angels and the saints
render to Jesus Christ in heaven.

Let us lift ourselves up to
heaven, O my soul, and render
thanks to the Lord our God.
How just is it, O holy Father,
and how reasonable, to glorify
thee, to give thee thanks, at
all times and in all places, as
our benefactor and our God.
Through Jesus Christ, the angels and the virtues of the
heavens, the Cherubim and

Seraphim, emulate each other in celebrating thy glory and singing thy praises. May I, great God, unite my heart and voice with their celestial songs, and cry with them: Holy, holy, holy, Lord God of Sabaoth. Heaven and earth are full of thy glory. Hosanna in the highest. Blessed is he that cometh in the name of the Lord, and will shortly descend upon this altar.

After the Preface follows the Canon of the Mass, or the most sacred and solemn part of this divine service, which is read with a low voice.

AT THE MEMENTO FOR THE LIVING.

O Father of mercy, graciously receive this most holy sacrifice which we offer to thee by the hands of thy priest, in union with that which thy beloved Son offered to thee on the cross. Look down on thy Christ, thy dearest and only begotten Son, « in whom thou art always well pleased, » and by the infinite merits of his incarnation, nativity, tears, labours, sufferings, and death, have mercy upon me, and upon all those for whom I ought to pray (*here name*) my parents, friends, benefactors, relations.

DEVOTIONS FOR MASS. 121

At the memento for the living.

I also beseech thee to defend, prosper, and extend thy holy Church, to pour down thy blessing upon our chief pastor the Pope, upon the Bishops and the priests. Give all those whom thou hast called to the sacred ministry the spirit of knowledge, zeal, and piety, especially him (*or* them) whom thou hast set over us. Bless us all, O Lord; may we all know thee, may we all please thee perfectly, may we all love and glorify thee.

WHEN THE PRIEST HOLDS HIS HANDS OVER THE CHALICE.

Then the priest extends his hands, according to the ancient ceremony of sacrifices, over the bread and wine, wich are to be changed into the body and blood of Christ, and begs that God would accept of this oblation, which he makes in the name of the whole Church, and that he would grand us peace in this life, and eternal salvation in the next.

124   DEVOTIONS FOR MASS.

When the Priest holds his hand over the chalice.

WHEN THE PRIEST SIGNS THE OBLATION.

(*Here the bell is rung.*)

Give ear, we beseech thee, O Lord, to the prayers of thy servant, who is here appointed to make this oblation in our behalf; and grand that it may obtain all those blessings which he asks for us.

The priest then proceeds to the consecration, first of the bread into the body of our Lord, and then of the wine into his blood; wich consecration is made by Christ's own words, pronounced in his name and person by the priest, and is the most essential part of this sacrifice; because thereby the body and blood of Christ are really exhibited and presented to God, and Christ is mystically immolated.

126 DEVOTIONS FOR MASS.

When the Priest signs the oblation.

At the consecration bow down your body and soul in solemn adoration. Make an act of faith in the real presence of your Saviour's body and blood, soul and divinity, under the sacramental veils. Offer your whole self to him, and through him to his Father. Beg that your heart and soul may be happily changed into him.

AT THE ELEVATION OF THE HOST.

(*Here the bell is rung thrice.*)

Hail, Incarnate Word. sacrificed for me and all mankind! Hail, holy Victim, offered once for us upon the altar of the Cross, and still daily offered upon our altars tho the end of time. I bless thee, I adore thee, I love thee. Oh, let not this sacrifice be offered for me in vain, but make me now and for ever wholly thine.

DEVOTIONS FOR MASS.   129

At the elevation of the Host.

AT THE ELEVATION OF THE CHALICE.

(Here also the bell is rung thrice.)

Hail, sacred Blood, flowing from the wounds of Jesus Christ, and washing away the sins of the world! Oh, cleanse, sanctify, and preserve my soul, that nothing may ever separate me from thee.

DEVOTIONS FOR MASS. 131

At the elevation of the chalice.

Then the Priest proceeds to the Memento, or Commemoration of the Dead, saying:

AT THE MEMENTE FOR THE DEAD.

I offer thee again, O Lord, this holy sacrifice of the body and blood of thy only Son, in behalf of the faithful departed, and in particular for the souls of (*here name those you wish to pray for*). To these, O Lord, and to all that rest in Christ, grant, we beseech thee, a place of refreshment, light, and peace. Through the same Christ our Lord. Amen.

After this Memento, or Commemoration of the Dead, the priest, raising his voice d striking his breast, says.

DEVOTIONS FOR MASS. 133

At the memente for the dead.

« Nobis quoque peccatoribus — And also to us sinners, » &c., humbly craving mercy and pardon for his sins, and to be admitted to some part and society with the apostles and martyrs, through Jesus Christ.

A PRAYER AT THE NOBIS QUOQUE PECCATORIBUS.

Be merciful to us sinners, O Lord, we beseech thee, and of thy great goodnes grant us all pardon and peace. We ask this in the name of thy dear Son, who liveth and reigneth eternally with thee, and in that form of prayer which he himself hath taught us.

A prayer at the nobis quoque peccatoribus.

AT THE LITTLE ELEVATION.

With grateful hearts we now call to mind, O Lord, the sacred mysteries of thy passion and death, of thy resurrection and ascension. Here is thy body that was broken, here is thy blood that was shed for us; of which these exterior signs are but the figures, and yet in reality contain the substance. Now we truly offer thee, O Lord, that pure and holy Victim which thou hast been pleased to give us; of wich all the other sacrifices were but so many types and figures.

DEVOTIONS FOR MASS. 137.

At the little elevation.

AT THE PATER NOSTER.

At the « Pater noster, » join with the priest in that sacred prayer; and at the conclusion of it, beg with him to be delivered from all evils, past, present, and to come; and by the intercession of the Blessed Virgin, and all the saints, to be secured from sin, and all disturbances, through Jesus Christ our Lord.

Our Father, who art in heaven, hallowed be thy name : thy kingdom come : thy will be done on earth, as it is in heaven. Give us this day our daily bread : and forgive us our trespasses, as we forgive them that trespass against us; and lead us not into temptation; but deliver us from evil. Amen.

DEVOTIONS FOR MASS. 139

At the Pater noster.

AT THE BREAKING OF THE HOST.

After this the priest breaks the host over the chalice, in remembrance of Christ's body being broken for us upon the cross; and he puts a small particle of the host into the chalice, praying that the peace of the Lord may be always with us.

At the breaking of the host, say:

Thy body was broken, and thy blood was shed for us; grant that the commemoration of this holy mystery may obtain for us peace, and that those who receive it may find everlasting rest.

Then kneeling down, and rising up again, the priest says, « Agnus Dei, » &c.

At the breaking of the Host.

THE PRIEST PUTS PART OF THE HOST INTO THE CHALICE.

Thy body was broken, and thy blood shed for us : grant that the commemoration of thy holy mystery may obtain for us peace : and that those who receive it may find ever lasting rest.

O Lord our God, pure and spotless Victim, who only canst satisfy the justice of an offended God ; vouchsafe to make me partaker of the merits of thy sacrifice. What lessons of humility, meekness, charity and patience dost thou not

The Priest puts part of the Host into the chalice.

give me! Impress these virtues upon my heart, that it may be to thee a pleasant habitation, wherein thou mayest repose, as in an abode of peace.

DEVOTIONS FOR MASS.

AT THE AGNUS DEI.

Lamb of God, who takest away the sins of the world, have mercy on us.

Lamb of God, who takest away the sins of the world, have mercy on us.

Lamb of God, who takest away the sins of the world, grant us peace.

The priest then says three short prayers, by way of preparation for receiving the blessed sacrament; then kneeling down, and rising again, he takes up the host, and striking his breast, he says thrice, « Domine, non sum dignus, &c.

At the « Domine, non sum dignus, » say thrice:

Lord, I am not worthy that

146 DEVOTIONS FOR MASS.

At the Agnus Dei.

thou shouldst enter under my roof; but only say the word, and my soul shall be healed.

If you do not yet communicate, say here:

Though I cannot now receive this sacrament, O most loving Jesus, I adore thee with a lively faith, who are present in this sacrament by virtue of thy infinite power, wisdom, and goodness. — All my hope is in thee; I love thee, O Lord, with all my heart, who hast so loved me; and I desire to receive thee spiritually; come therefore, to me, O dear Lord, and fill my soul with thy presence; and I beseech thee to prepare my soul for that happy time when I shall be permitted to

AT THE COMMUNION.

approach thy altar, and partake of the bread of life; deliver me from all sin, give me strength against my temptations, and make me always obedient to thy commands; and let me never be separated from thee, my Saviour. who, with the Father and the Holy Ghost, livest and reignest, one God, for ever and ever. Amen.

After the Communion, the priest takes the ablution of wine and water into the chalice, in order to consume whatever may remain of the consecrated species.

DEVOTIONS FOR MASS. 149

At the Communion.

PRAYER DURING THE ABLUTION.

I adore thy goodness, O gracious Lord, in admitting me to be present, this day at that holy sacrifice, where thou art both priest and victim. Oh, make me always sensible of so great a blessing, and grant me a part in the fruits of thy death and passion.

Prayer during the ablution.

AFTER COMMUNION.

Then covering the chalice, he goes to the book, and reads a versicle of Holy Scripture called the Communion.

FOR THE COMMUNION.

One thing I have asked of the Lord, this will I seek after, that I may dwell in the house of the Lord all the days of my life. Taste and see that the Lord is sweet, blessed is the man, that hopeth in him.

DEVOTIONS FOR MASS. 153

After Communion.

AT DOMINUS VOBISCUM.

The priest then turns to the people, with the usual salutation, « Dominus vobiscum, » and returning to the book, reads the collects or prayers called the Post Communion.

DEVOTIONS FOR MASS. 155

At Dominus vobiscnm.

AT THE LAST COLLECT.

Most gracious God, Father of mercy, grant, I beseech thee, that this adorable sacrifice of the blessed body and blood of thy son, our Lord Jesus Christ, may obtain for us mercy, and the remission of all our sins. Amen.

DEVOTIONS FOR MASS. 157

At the last Collect.

AT THE LAST DOMINUS VOBISCUM.

After this the priest again greets the people with « Dominus vobiscum; » and gives them leave to depart with « Ite, missa est, » the clerk answering, « Deo gratias—Thanks be to God. »

DEVOTIONS FOR MASS. 159

At the last Dominus vobiscum.

The priest then makes the last offering of the Mass, and turns to give his blessing.

AT THE BLESSING.

I thank thee O Lord, for making me a Christian and a Catholic; pour forth thy blessing and thy grace upon me that I may serve thee with fidelity and perseverance.

DEVOTIONS FOR MASS. 161

At the Blessing.

THE GOSPEL OF ST. JOHN.

In the beginning was the Word, and the Word was with God, ant the Word was God. The same was in the beginning with God. All things were made by him; and without him was made nothing that was made. In him was life, and the life was the light of men ; and the light shineth in darkness, and the darkness did not comprehend it. There was a man sent from God, whose name was John. This man came for a witness, to give testimony of the light, that all men might

believe through him. He was not the light, but was to give testimony of the light. That was the true light, which enlighteneth every man that cometh into this world. He was in the world, and the world was made by him, and the world knew him not. He came unto his own, and his own received him not. But as many as received him, he gave them power to be made the sons of God; to them that believe in his name, who are born, not of blood, nor of the will of the flesch, nor of the will of man, but of God. And *the word mas made flesh (here kneel down),* and dwelt among us (and we saw his glory, as it were, of the only-begotten of the Father), full of grace and truth.

PRAYER AFTER MASS.

I return thee most hearty thanks, O my God, through Jesus Christ thy Son, that thou hast been pleased to deliver him up to death for us, and to give us his body and blood, both as a sacrament and a sacrifice, in these holy mysteries, at which thou hast permitted me to assist this day. May all heaven and earth bless and praise thee for all thy mercies. Pardon me, O Lord, all thee distractions and negligences which I have been guilty of this day in thy sight; and let me not depart without thy blessing. I desire from this moment to give up myself wholly into thy hands ; and I beg that my thoughts, words, and actions may always tend to thy glory, through the same Jesus Christ our Lord. Amen.

PRAYER WHEN PREPARING FOR FIRST COMMUNION.

O divine Jesus! who when on earth didst receive children with the tenderness of a father, and didst command that they should not be forbidden to approach thy sacred person, I see that thou art in the holy Eucharist the same God of goodness and mercy; and thou invitest me not only to approach thee, but to receive thy adorable body and blood. I rejoice to think that this happiness will soon be mine, and I bless thee for thy goodness in bestowing upon us, weak and sinful children, the most precious of all thy gifts. O my God, I beseech thee to prepare my soul by thy grace for so great a mystery; and permit not, I most earnestly beseech thee, that I should receive unworthily. O Lord, I depend not upon myself, but upon thee alone, for avoiding so great an evil, and for acquiring all the dispositions necessary for receiving thee worthily. Give me grace to profit by all the advantages of religious instruction which I enjoy; enable me, by a good confession, to purify my heart from every stain of sin; and may my first communion be to me, and to all who are to receive with me, a happy pledge of our eternal union with thee in heaven.

INSTRUCTIONS FOR CONFESSION.

Take time to examine your conscience before confession. Call on the Holy Spirit in the following prayer to assist you, and beg the grace of God to know your sins, and be heartilly sorry for them.

O DIVINE Spirit of truth, enlighten my mind, and bring to my remembrance all the sins I have committed, and give me a true sorrow and contrition for them.

Examination of Conscience, in form of Accusation.

Have I, trough negligence, omitted to perform the whole of my last penance?

Gone to school against my will; come late through my own fault; lost my time in laughing, talking, and playing; hindered others from improving;

turned my thoughts to other things, when I should have listened to instruction; not learned my lessons or catechisms, or learned them badly, or out of vanity, and not from a desire to please God and do my duty.

Omitted prayer morning or evening; prayed to God out of mere custom, or because obliged; prayed hastily, in a disrespectful posture, looking about me, without devotion, or sincerely desiring to obtain what I prayed for, or even reflecting that I was speaking to God.

Wanted reverence in church; laughed, or spoken there without necessity, or made a noise, or slept.

Gone to church from a wrong motive, such as to meet friends, put on a new dress, &c.

Despised or been unkind to the poor —neglected to do good to my neighbour when I had the opportunity.

Taken the holy name of God in vain;

not offered up my actions to God, nor done them with the intention of pleasing him; not been grateful for his blessings; not feared to displease him, but exposed myself to the danger of offending him.

Not being sorry for my sins, or laboured to correct my bad habits, or made endeavours to advance in piety; not been submissive to the will of God, or borne sickness or crosses with patience, and as the punishment of my sins.

Been selfish, studied my own interest, and been attentive only to gratify my own inclinations.

Been proud and vain, fond of pleasure and dress, and of being admired.

Been passionate, and cried with vexation when humbled, despised, or contradicted.

Been obstinate, disobeyed my parents, or those who have authority over me, or are charged with my education; and, when forced to obey, have done it against my will ; made insolent answers, and not respected, but spoken ill of them, and despised their advice.

Been insupportable by my ill temper. Been wanting in kindness far my brothers or sisters, or companions; not borne with their defects, or assisted them in their employments ; quarelled with them, or with my companions; told tales of them without necessity, out of revenge or pride, that I might be preferred before them.

Dwelt with pleasure on sinful thoughts; looked at any thing indecent, such as pictures, &c.; said, done, or consented to any thing contrary to modesty; been curious to know evil; listened to wicked discourse.

Eaten food to excess. Taken things belonging to others without their knowledge or consent. Coveted things belonging to my companions. Been unjust in my dealings with them—taken advantage of their ignorance, &c. Been selfish, or over fond of what I possessed, unwilling to allow a share to others. Considered riches as a great happiness.

Envied my brothers, sisters, or companions, when they were esteemed, praised, or enjoyed any advantage which I did not possess.

Not watched over my tongue—given way to slander or detraction. Told lies to excuse myself, or in boasting, or out of a bad habit. Exaggered, or made false excuses.

Stolen or wantonly injured the property of others.

Partaken of the sins of others, by doing, approving, or laughing at them.

Remember that the priest holds the place of Jesus Christ : present yourself, therefore, at the confessionnal with the utmost recollection and humility, on your knees, yet with confidence and sincerity, like the sick who discover their disorders to their physician, and as children who speak to a kind and compassionate father. When the confessor makes the sign of the cross, then with great respect ask his blessing in a low but distinct voice, saying thus : « Pray, father, give me your blessing, for I have sinned. » Then say the Confiteor, till you come to the words, « through my exceeding great fault ; » stop, and say to your confessor. « It was (so long) since I came to confession, since which I accuse myself, » &c.

Act of Contrition.

O merciful God! I am sorry, from the bottom of my heart, for these, and all my other sins. It grieves me, that I have so offended thee. I implore thy clemency, and humbly hope to receive thy pardon. I offer to thee, in satisfaction for all my sins, of thought, word, and deed, and especially those I have committed this day, the sacred merits of thy beloved Son, Jesus Christ. I firmly purpose never more wilfully to offend thee. I resolve, from this moment to endeavour to love and serve thee better than I have hitherto done. Confirm me in this good purpose, to the glory of thy name, and the eternal salvation of my soul. Amen.

Listen with submission and humillity to your confessor, and answer him with truh and simplicity. When you have finished accusing yourself, say the rest of the Confiteor, p. 36. Then make an Act of Contrition.

Be particularly attentive to the penance imposed on you. Fulfil it as soon and as exactly as possible. Do not tell others, or listen to what they have told in confession. After confession, take time to reflect on your confessor's advice, and make a resolution to serve God with more fidelity in future. For that purpose say the Acts of Faith, Hope, and the Love of God, as in your Catechism, or at p. 38 of this book, and the following prayer for renewing your baptismal vows : but consider well, that it is not enough to recite these acts, unless we have in our hearts the sentiments they express; for it is not by the lips, but by the affections of the heart, that we can repent of our faults, or show our faith, hope, love, and adoration to God.

A Thanksgiving after Confession.

I give thee tanks, O Lord Jesus,

that thou hast been pleased to cleanse me from the stains of my sins. Blessed be thy Name, O Lord, who rejectest none that come unto thee with true repentance, but receivest them into thy favour, and numberest them with thy children. I acknowledge and adore thy mercy, and dedicate myself wholly to thy service hereafter. O, grant that for the time to come I may abhor sin more than death itself, and avoid all such occasions and companies as have unhappily brought me to it. This I resolve to do, by the aid of thy divine grace, without which I can do nothing. Grant, O Lord, that I may be able to keep these my resolutions, for without thee I am nothing but weakness and sin. Supply also, by thy mercy, whatever defects have been in this my confession, and give me grace to be now and always a true penitent, through the same Jesus Christ, thy Son. Amen.

A *Prayer for renewing our Baptismal Vows.*

I return thee thanks, O Almighty God, for having drawn me out of a state of darkness into thine admirable ligt. I was, alas! dead in sin, and thou, who art rich in mercy, didst restore me to life in Jesus Christ; thou hast made me a partaker of the divine nature, by the infusion of thy Holy Spirit into my soul at the baptismal font, that, purified by thy grace, I might become thy heir, and inherit eternal life. O bountiful Father, how great is my obligation to love thee, who hast first given me such admirable proofs of thy love! Ik will therefore no longer love the world, nor that which it contains; but, having the happiness of being a member of Christ, I will crucify the flesh with all its evil inclinations. Grant, O heavenly, Father, that I may always live by thy Spirit, and appear in thy sight as a child newly born in thy grace. Banish all kind of malice, pride, and deceit from my heart, that, anxious to feed on the pure spiritual milk of thy word, I may increase unto salvation. Oh, may I never grieve thy Holy Spirit by sin, but grant that, through thy grace, I may be ever fruitful in good works; so that, living in this world in a manner worthy of thee, I may at length obtain admittance into that kingdom of everlasting glory for which I was created, Through Jesus Christ our Lord. Amen.

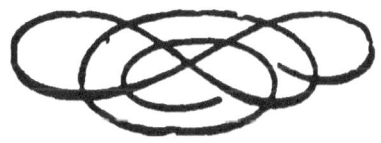

INSTRUCTIONS FOR COMMUNION.

FIRTS COMMUNION.

THE greatest blessing which our Divine Redeemer left us, when he ascended to his Father was the Sacrament of his Body and Blood. « I will not leave you orphans. » « Lo, I am with you all days even to the consummation of the world. » He becomes our spiritual food : in the sacrament of his love he lavishes every blessing upon us. during our lives we may frequently receive our Lord in the Holy Eucharist, but the graces which we receive in our First Communion are seldom renewed. It forms an epoch in ourselves to which we should look forward with a holy awe, and prepare for with every care. In our prayers we should bear it in mind, and when we see others communicate, envy them with a holy envy, and like the prophets who sighed for our Saviour's coming frequently, implore him to hasten the time when you shall at last approach the awful Sacrement.

« Come quickly, Lord Jesus, come quickly. »
« Lord I shall be filled, when thy glory shall appear. »

INSTRUCTIONS FOR COMMUNION. 179

As the time approaches renew your fervor, attend with great punctuality the instructions given in the church of seek others at home : do not so pre-occupy yourself with your confession as to leave no thought for your communion, and above all choose some fault and endeavor to overcome it by that happy day, in order to offer to your Lord a sacrifice pleasing in his sight.

After having made your confession with due preparation and a firm resolution to lead a new life, give all your thougths to your Communion. Let all your reading and prayers refer to this, and pay frequent visits to the Blessed Sacrament.

GENERAL PREPARATION.

On the morning of your first Communion, and of all that follow it, rise early and give your first thougths to God : think only of the guest whom you are to receive. Spend such time as may be left you before mass in reading, prayer or meditating on the goodness of Our Lord to all who love him : and of the graces which we may expect if we receive him worthily and with fervor of spirit.

PRAYERS BEFORE COMMUNION.

I FIRMLY believe, O my Divine Jesus' that Thou, True God and True Man art really present in the Blessed Sacrament of the Altar. I believe that *there* are Thy Body, Thy Blood, Thy Soul, and Thy Divinity. I believe that *there* Thou communicatest Thyself to us, makest us partakers of the fruit of Thy Passion, and givest us a pledge of eternal life. I acknowledge these truths; I believe these wonders; I adore the power that has wrought them, the same power that said, « Be light made, and light was made. » I submit my sense and reason to Thy divine authority. I praise and glorify Thy infinite goodness which hath prepared this heavenly banquet for the food and nourishment of my soul. Blessed be Thy name forever. Accept my homage : accept O my God, my most hearty thanks.

Who is He thou art about to receive? O my soul, be still and attentive. Who is He thou art going to receive? Thy God! thy Redeemer! Who, for love of thee, shed torrrents of blood during His agony in the garden of Gethsemani! Who, for love of thee, suffered His sacred head to be pierced by a crown of thorns, and His virginal flesch to be rent and torn at the pillar with whips and scourges! Who, for love of thee, snffered Himself to be clothed in a purple garment, and derided as a mock king, with a reed for His sceptre! Who, for love of thee, suffered His sacred hands and feet to be fastened with sharp nails to the wood of the cross! In fine, Who, for love of thee, hung thereon, in the most ignominious manner, between two thieves, suffering for the space of three hours the most excruciating pains and tortures, and at last expired for thy redemption! After such stupendous instances of Thy love to man, who can refuse a return of love to Thee, Lord Jesus? I love Thee, O my God: and ardently wish, that as every breath I draw is an increase of my life, so it may be of my love for Thee, till at last I love Thee in the manner Thou Thyself requirest, that is, « with my whole heart, with my whole soul, with all my mind, and with all my strength; » for Thou art the God of my heart, and the life of my soul; Thou art my treasure, my joy, my comfort, my support, my strength, my armor, my defence, my only hope and comfort in this place of banishment and vale of tears, and the supreme object of my happiness in heaven.

Immediately before going up to the Altar :

O most holy Virgin Mary, and all ye blessed Angels and Saints of God, I humbly beg the assistance of your prayers and intercession, that I may, with a clean heart and pure conscience, approach the Holy of Holies, and receive, this divine Sacrament with such reverence and humility as may be for my soul's salvation. Amen.

When about to communicate, endeavor to excite within yourself the utmost devotion. At the moment you receive the blessed Sacrament, reflect on the words pronounced by the Priest, *Corpus Domini nostri Jesu Christi custodiat animam tuam in vitam æternam. Amen.* » *May the Body of our Lord Jesus Christ preserve thy soul to life everlasting. Amen.* For they imply, that the end proposed in communicating is, not simply to maintain a certain regularity of conduct for a few days, weeks, or months but to persevere faithfully, to the very hour of death, in that state of grace to which a worthy participation of this divine Sacrament shall now raise you.

THANKSGIVING AFTER COMMUNION.

After Communion, spend, at least, a quarter of an hour in thanksgiving. Consider yourself as a living tabernacle, wherein resideth the Holy of Holies. Let this single reflection prevent all distractions, and keep your mind in the most perfect composure and recollection. Pray, therefore, mentally for some time, and then, rather with your heart than with your lips, address yourself thus to your God :

BEHOLD, my desires are satisfied, my hunger is satiated; my God has come to visit me; Jesus has entered into me; I am no longer my own, but now I belong to Jesus. Oh, infinite goodness of God, to enter the heart of one so vile and unworthy as myself! My soul, on what thinkest thou? Lo, thou art sanctified by Jesus, and transformed into Jesus. Thou and he are one. Oh, true and wonderful union! My soul, art thou yet silent? Dost thou not speak with thy God, whom thou hast within thee? Ah, unite all the affections of thy spirit, hide thyself in the sacred heart of thy Jesus, adore him and say: Thou art welcome, O dear Lord! Oh, how have I longed for this hour! But, alas, my sins have often caused thee to renew thy passion and death. Lord, what dost thou find in me but earthly love? O my God, art thou come to dwell with me? I could say to thee with St Pether, Depart from this sinful soul, for she is not worthy to contain a God. « Depart from me, for I am a sinful man, O Lord! » Go take up thine abode in some purer and more fervent soul than mine. But, no! my Well-beloved, depart not from me : for if thou goest away, I am lost. O God, my hope, I will not leave thee. O unite thee to my heart, and will live and die with thee. O Mary, O ye holy Angels, ye Saints, ye souls that love God, lend me your affections, that I may thus become a worthy companion of my Jesus.

ACTS OF THANKSGIVING.

The heavens are now open, the blessed Trinity regard thee with looks of love, since thou hast in thy bosom the object of their delight, Jesus Christ. Supplicate Mary, the Angels, the Saints, thy advocates with God, to obtain thee every grace. Do not, my soul, lose a moment of this precious time; treat of the important affair of thy eternal salvation alone. My soul, thou hast within thee an omnipotent Lord, a living Father, a faithful God. Ask and trust; he will enlarge thy heart, strengthen thy faith; he begins to give thee graces, heavenly graces, worthy of God to give.

My dear Redeemer, since thou art come to me, and dost invite me to pray to thee, hear me by the bowels of thy mercy. Grant me, O my Jesus, an increase of lively faith, hope, charity, and contrition. Grant me humility, purity, patience, and alle the virtues; extirpate every vice from my heart. Change this heart, so filled with the world, and give me a new heart altogether conformable to thy will, that I may always seek after thy greater glory, and that my affections may tend to thy love. « Create a clean heart in me, O God, and renew a right spirit within me. »

Holy Trinity, omnipotent God, hear my prayers. Thou wilt not deny me any grace now, although I am so unworthy, for I do not pray alone, but Jesus Christ is united with me : and though I deserve not to be heard, yet the merits of Jesus Christ, who prays with me, in me, and for me, thou wilt not refuse to listen to. Eternal Father remember the promise of Jesus, when he said, that whoever asked thee any thing in his name should be heard : « Amen, amen I say to you, if you ask the Father any thing in my name, he will give it you. »

ACT OF OFFERING.

It is but just, it is only an act of gratitude, O my Jesus, that I should give myself entirely to thee, since thou hast given thyself entirely to me. Let my eyes be thine, my ears thine, my taste thine. Thou hast sanctified my senses; let them, then, be all thine : let them no longer be opposed to thy divine and holy law, but act according to it in all things. Thou hast sanctified my memory; may it be ever mindful of thee. Thou hast sanctified my intellect; may it think on thee alone. Thou hast sanctified my will; may it be in harmony only with thine. To thee, then, with my whole heart do I offer, as a perpetual holocaust, my soul and body, my senses and my powers. Burn, o divine fire, all that is foreign to thee in me. Consume, O omnipotent Lord, all that is not thine. Amen.

But do not limit the devotion of this day do the foregoing prayers; consider it rather as entirely consecrated to Jesus Christ, that by this means you may literally accomplish the precept of the Holy Ghost : « Defraud not Thyself of the good day, and let not the part of a good gift overpass thee. » Recollect frequently this great action; and read some pious book to nourish and enliven a spirit of devotion.

INSTRUCTIONS FOR CONFIRMATION.

Confirmation is a Sacrement which gives us strength to perform our Christian duties, and persevere in the path which we have begun. Some will say that it is not absolutely necessary : but in this Sacrament we receive the Holy Ghost with all his gifts. Can we refuse it without danger? Look around and see the young who have fallen from the practice of their religious duties : who after years of fervor, are now years aloof from the sacraments. Ask whether they were confirmed, and you will find that they generally neglected or refused to prepare for this great Sacrament.

The preparation for confirmation is *first;* to be in a state of grace. « The Holy Spirit will not dwell in a soul defiled by sin. — *Second :* « To hunger and thirst after justice, » that is to have, an earnest longing and desire of receiving the Holy Ghost and his coming as the Apostles did by retirement and prayer.

As for your first Communion, endeavor to overcome some fault, or acquire some virtue to offer as a sacrifice to your God.

During the period of preparation, repeat frequently the hymns in honor of the Holy Ghost, and excite your fervor by ejaculatory prayers.

« Come, O Holy Ghost replenish my hert and enkindle in it the fire of thy divine love. »

PREPARATORY PRAYER BEFORE CONFIRMATION.

O God of infinite goodness! Who were graciously pleased at my baptism to make me Thy child, receive my fervent thanksgiving for all the favors bestowed on me from my birth to this moment, particulary for my being now ranked among those who are to be peculiarly consecrated to Thee by the Sacrament of Confirmation. Alas! my God, I am far from possessing those sentiments of faith, love, humility, and fervor which should now animate my soul; but it will be easy for Thee to grant them to me. I most sinserely detest every sin of my life, and every fault, or even imperfect inclination which may be an obstacle to the graces Thou desirest to bestow on Thy unworthy child. Do thou deign to purify me from every stain, by applying to my soul the infinite merits of Thy Death and Passion. I purpose most sincerely to serve Thee with fidelity from this day forward; but I feel that I am too weak to execute my resolution, if left to myself; therefore, I conjure Thee to impart to me Thy Holy Spirit, that, like the Apostles, I may be endued with strength from on high, and inspired with courage and resolution to prove myself in reality Thy follower. I desire to receive this most precious favor; but do Thou render this desire still more ardent, and accept, on my behalf, the fervent desires which animated the heart of Thy blessed Mother and the Apostles previous to the descent of the Holy Ghost, and let their perfect dispositions in every other respect atone and supply for my deficiencies.

PRAYER TO THE HOLY GHOST,

To beg the Descent of that Divine Spirit with His seven-fold Gifts.

O HEAVENLY Spirit! Whom I earnestly desire to receive in the Sachament of Confirmation, myrcifully deign to descend on me with all Thy gifts and graces. O eternal Light! O infinite Charity! O uncreated Wisdom, Who replenishest the hearts of the faithful, and kindlest in them the fire of Thy love! O holy Spirit! Who didst inspire the prophets, Who presidest over the Church, Who convertest sinners, and sanctifiest millions that listen to Thy inspirations, despise not my youth, my ignorance, and weakness. In a moment Thou canst enlighten the darkest understanding, and soften the hardest heart. O! come then into my heart; come, heavenly Spirit; and do not delay.

O sacred Virgin! Spouse of the Holy Ghost, Whose pure soul was the chosen tabernacle of that heavenly Spirit, and who above all creatures were plentifully enriched with his choicest gifts and graces, intercede for me, and by Thy powerful prayers prepare me for the happiness I so sincerly desire.

Glorious Apostles! who received the plentitude of the Divine Spirit, obtain for me by your prayers a share in the perfect dispositions, which prepared you to receive that consolatory Spirit.

CEREMONY OF CONFIRMATION.

On the morning of your Confirmation, renew with redoubled fervor your desire to be replenished with the Holy Ghost. Assist at the Holy Sacrifice of the Mass with particular devotion, and offer up the Adorable Victim of our Altars to atone for all the sins of your life, and to obtain any disposition which the all-seeing eye of God may discern to be still wanting in your heart.

After the holy Sacrifice is concluded, call to mind the explanation wich has been given you of each ceremony used in the administration of the Sacrament of Confirmation, that thereby you may recive it with more devotion and reverence ; then devoutly join in the prayers offered for you by the Bishop in administering the Sacrament. The ceremony is as follows :

First, the Bishop turning towards those to be confirmed, says :

« May the Holy Gost come down upon you, and the power of the Most High keep you from all sin.

R. Amen.

Signing himself with the sign of the † Cross, he goes on :

« *Bish.* Our help is in the name of the Lord.

R. Who made heaven and earth.

Bish. O Lord, hear my prayer.

R. And let my cry come unto Thee.

Bish. The Lord be with you.

« *R*. And with thy spirit. »

Then he extends his hands over those to be confirmed, and addresses a solemn prayer to the Éternal Father, begging, through Jesus Christ His divine Son, that He would send down His Holy Spirit, with all His gifts and graces, into their souls.

CONFIRMATION. 195

Then the Bishop, making the sign of the † Cross of the forehead of each of those who are to be confirmed with holy chrism, and calling him by the name he has chosen, says:

" (*N.*) I sign thee with the sign of the Cross, and confirm thee with the chrism of salvation, in the name of the Father †, and of the Son †, and of the Holy † Ghost. "

After wich, he gives the person confirmed a slight stroke on thee cheek, saying, at the same time, *Peace be with thee*.

As soon as you return to your place, after having been confirmed, raise your heart to God in sentiments of the most lively gratitude. Imagine you are among the Apostles after the descent of the Holy Ghost, and join most devoutly in the transports with which they gloriefied God. You need not be recommended to observe the most edifying recollection and modesty while the Bishop continues to administer the Sacrament. The adorable guest you have received will excite you to sentiments of the most profound veneration and humility, particularly when you consider how unworthy you are of His presence You may employ those few moments in reflecting on your happiness, and thank God for it in any terms your devotion may suggest. The sentiments of the heart are at all times preferable to any set form, but more particulary at a time when you may humbly hope that they are suggested by the Divine Spirit of God Himself.

After all have been confirmed, the Bishop washes his hands. Then, standing, and turned towards the Althar he says the following prayers, in which you should devoutly join.

« *Bish.* Show us, O Lord, Thy mercy.

« *R.* And grant us Thy salvation.

« *Bish.* O Lord, hear my prayer.

« *R.* And let my cry come unto Thee.

« *Bish.* The Lord be with you.

« *R.* And with thy spirit. »

Bishop. Let us pray.

O God, Who gavest the Holy Ghost to thy Apostles, and hast been pleased to ordain that by them and their successors that same Divine Spirit should be given to the rest of the faithful, mercifully look down upon what we Thy servants have done, and grant that the hearts of these Thy faithful, whose force-

CONFIRMATION. 197

heads we have anointed with the sacred chrism, and signed with the sign of the Cross, may, by the same Holy Spirit coming down unto them, and by His vouchsafing to dwell in them, be made the temple of His glory, Who with the Father and the Holy Ghost liveth and reigneth God, world without end. Amen.

Then the Bishop concludes the ceremony by giving a solemn Benediction to all present, in these words :

« Behold, thus shall every man be blessed who feareth the Lord. May the Lord bless † you out of Sion, that you may see the good things of Jerusalem all the days of your life, and that you may live with Him for all eternity. Amen. "

As you have reason to trust in the mercy of God, that you did not fail in any of the essential dispositions for Confirmation, you have now only to profit by the great gift you have received, and to let every one see that this Sacrament has produced in you the fruits of the Holy Ghost, viz : Charity, Joy, Peace, Patience, Longanimity, or Perseverance, Goodness, Benignity, Mildness, Fidelity, or Sincerity, Modesty, Continency, and Chastity. You know the meaning of those virtues, and the method of exercising them ; but you should particularly attend to those which peculiarly appertain to your present age ; such as *Charity*, which does not merely consist in loving God, but also in loving your neighbor for His sake ; — *Patience*, which is exercised on a thousand little occasions that too often serve to irritate those who did not correct their tempers in their youth and *Mildness*, which is so peculiarly necessary and attractive in young persons ; — *Modesty*, that amiable virtue, which renders those who are so happy as to possess it silent and retiring, diffident of their abilities and opinions, and reserved in their manners. Beg them, most earnestly, from the heavenly Spirit you have received, and also implore the other fruits of His holy presence, particularly *Charity*, which is the perfection of every virtue, and which in itself contains them all. For this intention, and in thanksgiving for the inestimable advantages you have recived, say devoutly the following prayer every day for a week or fortnight after Confirmation.

A PRAYER AFTER CONFIRMATION.

Is it possible, O my good and merciful Creator, that Thou hast so far overlooked my misery and unworthiness, as to make my soul the tabernacle of Thy Holy Spirit! Can I believe that I am now honored with the presence and enriched wit the gifts and graces of the Holy Ghost? Yes, I firmly hope that Thou hast not been deaf to my petitions; I hope I am now in possession of that sacred gift I so ardently desired. O my God! accept the praises of Thy Angels and Saints in thanksgiving for Thy unbounded mercies in my regard May the blessed Mother of Thy Divine Son, and the glorious choir of Apostles, thank Thee for me. May the Cross of Jesus Christ, with which my forehead has been signed, defend me from all my ennemies, and save me at the last day. May the inward unction of sanctifying grace, figured by the chrism with which

I have been anointed, penetrate my soul, soften my heart, strenghten my will, and consecrate my whole being to Thy service.

O heavenly Spirit! third person of the Adorable Trinity! Whom I have received, and most fervently adore, deign to take eternal possesion of my soul; create and maintain therein the purity and sanctity which becomes Thy temple. O Spirit of *Wisdom!* preside over all my thoughts, words, ands actions, from this hour to the moment of my death. Spirit of *Understanding!* enlighten and teach me. Spirit of *Counsel!* direct my youth and inexperience. Spirit of *Fortitude!* strenghten my weakness. Spirit of *Knowledge!* instruct my ignorance. Spirit of *Piety!* make me fervent in good works. Spirit of *Fear!* restrain me from all evil, Let all my works be fruits of *Charity!* infuse into my heart the *joy* of a good conscience, and teach me to delight in the service of God, and to despise the false joys of the world. Give me grace to preserve *Peace* with God, my neighbor, and myself :—give me *Patience* to bear with all the ills of this life;—make me *persevere* in the service of God, and enable me to act on all occassions with *Goodness, Benignity, Mildness* and *Fidelity.* Let the heavenly virtues of *Modesty* and *Purity* adorn the temple Thou hast chosen for Thy abode. O Spirit of Purity! by Thy all-powerful grace preserve my soul from the misfortune of sin, wich for all eternity will be distinguished by the double title and sacred character of a Christian by Baptism, and a soldier of Jesus Christ by the Sacrament of Confirmation. Amen.

PIOUS PRACTICES,

IN HONOUR OF

THE SACRED HEART OF JESUS.

THIS practice, in honour of the Sacred Heart of Jesus, is divided into nine different offices, compiled from the heavenly lights, which our Lord communicated to his servant, Ven. Marguerite Mary Alacoque, a nun of the Order of the Visitation. By this practice, without multiplying vocal prayers or exterior practices, we may pay to this divine Heart a continual interior adoration, which a single person, howsoever fervent, would not be able to perform.

1st. On the Thursday preceding the first Friday of every month, the nine Offices of which this devotion consists, are distributed to nine persons, and each endeavors to acquit himself of his Office with all possible exactness until the next month.

2d. The first Friday of every month is to be distinguished from the rest by the fervor with which all our actions ought to be animated. Therefore — as our Saviour enjoined to the Ven. Marg. Mary, in her live, all will receive the Holy Communion with the leave of their respective Superior or spiritual Director, and renew the act of consecration.

3d. Every one, to the better accomplishing of his office, will strive in all the services he shall render to the Sacred Heart, to unite himself to the choir of blessed Spirits indicated in the Office itself, and make with them that mystical association which the Ven Margaret made with so great a profit to her soul, in order that they may supply our deficiencies, and fill our places in the hours of sleep, and in all others, whatever may be our impediments ; thus the Sacred Heart will be perpetually adored.

4th. And because the purest Heart of MARY is, after the Sacred Heart of Jesus, the most amiable and lovely, and bears a greater resemblance to it, all the associates will possess a cordial and tender devotion to this Sovereingn Queen, honoring Her to their utmost, especially on her principal feasts, and on the first Saturday of every month, and joining their actions and affections to those of this most innocent Virgin, in all the pious acts which they may exhibit to the divine Heart, for it is the most efficacious way to preserve and spread the devotion to the Sacred Heart of Jesus.

5th. The greatest service which all have to present to the most Sacred Heart of Jesus, and the chief fruit to be proposed or intended in the execution of this pious exercise, is the exact observance of all our rules, and duties of our state ; bearing constantly in mind the words of Jesus Christ to the Ven. Marg. Mary : « Thou canst not do any thing more agreeable to me than to run on with a constant fidelity and sincerity in the way of thy rules, in which the least defects are great in my sight ; and a religious person deceives himself, and withdraws far from me, when he thinks to please me, without the exact observance of his rules. »

6th. To connect more strictly the bond of Charity, which unites in the Sacred Heart of Jesus those that practice this devotion, each of them will pray every day for his companions, asking of the Sacred Heart that its love be increased in all, and that none become cold, or withdraw himself from this happy union. To this purpose it will be expedient to excite one another, and propagate, by every means in their power, the reign of the Sacred Heart.

7th. When any one has to separate from his companions, he will thereby not cease to belong to this pious union of special worshippers of the divine Heart, provided he proceed in performing the spiritual exercises.

8th. To avoid all scruples, it is to be observed, that whatever has been said, either in respect to the nine Offices, or to the foregoing acts or exercises, is always, and in every circumstance understood not to be binding. The love of the Sacred Heart alone, and the band of this sweet union, are the end and motive of whatever is proposed.

FIRST OFFICE.
PROMOTER.

THE Promoter of the devotion to the Sacred Heart of Jesus shall beg of the Eternal Father, that he would enlighten all men, in order that they may know it; and of the Holy Ghost, that he would make our hearts earnest in its love: and of the Blessed Virgin, that she would employ her intercession, to obtain that the influence of this divine Heart may be experienced by those who implore its mercy. During the day, he shall frequently retire into the sacred recesses of the divine Heart, and unite himself to it by the warmest affection ; and to honour it the better by his Office, he shall join himself in spirit with the choir of the *Thrones*. Moreover, he shall once visit the Most Holy Sacrament for the benefit of the Community or Confraternity, praying through the merits of this Divine Heart, that it allone would reign over all hearts, according to its loving designs. Finally, he shall say five : *Glories to the Father*, &c. *His virtue* ought to consist either in seeking to induce some person to practice the devotion of the Sacred Heart of Jesus, or to increase the fervor of those who already possess it, and for this intention he shall pray at least five times every day. Very happy sall he be, to whose lot this office sall have fallen, because our Saviour said « He would himself be Mediator between him and his divine Father. »

(Ven. Mary Alacoque.)

MAXIM :—As he sins grievously who induces others into guilty actions, so it is very laudable for one to strive by prayer and good works to lead others to a holy life and pious practices.

ASPIRATIONS.

Oh, sweetest Heart of Jesus! I implore
That I may ever love thee, more and more.

PRAYER.

Through Thy infinite goodness, grant, oh, my amiable Jesus! that all men may know the unparalleded excellence of thy Sacred Heart; and having trampeled under foot the world's deceitful pleasures, they may taste the unalterable delights which thou has prepared for those who sincerely love thee. AMEN.

PRAYER TO THE BLESSED TRINITY.

To be said daily by all the members.

O! Holy Trinity, one God! I offer to Thee in union with the merits of our Lord Jesus Christ, all my prayers, actions and sufferings of this day for Thy greater glory and the accomplishment of Thy holy will; in honour of the Blessed Virgin Mary, my holy Angel Guardian, and all my patron Saints, for the propagation of the devotion to the Sacred Heart of Jesus and Mary, in ful remission and satisfaction for my sins, for the conversion of sinners and the perseverance of the just; for the gaining of indulgences; for the repose of the souls in purgatory; for the spiritual profit and perfection of the members of our confraternity, and for all those for whom I am bound to pray, in thanksgiving for all the graces which Thou hast hitherto conferred om me, or that Thou wilt hereafter bestow on me, through the merits of Jesus Christ, our Lord. Amen.

PRAYER TO THE B. V. MARY.

To be said every day by all the members.

O, my Mistress! O, my Mother! I offer myself entirely to thee, and in order to approve myself devoted to thee, I consecrate to thee, this day my sight, my hearing, my speech, my heart, my whole person.

Since, therefore, I am thine, Oh! good Mother! preserve me, defend me, as thy property and possession.

ASPIRATION IN EVERY TEMPTATION.

O! Mary! O! my Mother! remember that I am thine. Preserve me, defend me, as thy property and possession.

SECOND OFFICE.

REPAIRER.

The Repairer shall, in a particular manner be obliged very humbly to beg pardon of God, for the injuries which are offered to him in the Most Holy Sacrament of the Altar. During the day, he shall frequently retire into the most Sacred Heart of Jesus, to satisfy the Divine Majesty, so much offended and abused. On this account, he shall invoke the choir of the Angels, who are called Powers, that they would assist him to compensate Jesus Christ for masses unworthily celebrated, and communions lukewarmly made by the souls which are specially consecrated to him, and even for the faults of the community, or confraternity, which might have been more displeasing to his divine Heart. With this aim, also, he shall once visit the Most Holy Sacrament, and make an act of reparation every Friday of the month, and particularly on the first Friday, he shall set forth his love toward the Sacred Heart of Jesus, by redoubling his fervor, and rendering to it particular homages, according as he will be inspired by his devotion.

His virtue will consist in a complete and faithful discharge of all the duties that concern his state; and in overcoming all human respects, should he meet with any; and every day he shall renew this resolution five times.

MAXIM: — He that shall engage himself to repair the abuses offered by others to the Divine Justice, may rest assured that the Lord will more and more forgive him the punishments due to his own sins, and will make him enjoy the sweet effects of his mercy.

ASPIRATIONS.

O, sweetest Heart of Jesus, I implore
That I may ever love thee, more and more.

PRAYER.

Thy Heart, O, my Jesus! is a treasure, the key of which is deposited in the hands of Confidence, Ah! grant that we may know the inestimable value of it. Amen.

Say the prayers to the Blessed Trinity, and the B. V. Mary, as before, pp. 207, 208.

SACRED HEART OF JESUS. 211

THIRD OFFICE.
ADORER.

THE Adorer, by his frequent interior adorations to the Most Holy Trinity, united with the praises which the most Sacred Heart of Jesus offers to it, shall endeavor to atone for men's forgetfulness of God. During the day, he shall oftentimes rejoice in the eternal praises which are sung by the blessed in heaven : Holy, Holy, Holy, is the Lord Almighty ; and often also shall sing it himself with the choir of Dominations, presenting at the same time to the august Heart of Jesus the good works which are done throughout the world, with the intention of consecrating them to its greater glory. He shall visit the Most Holy Sacrement on the part of the community, begging for each individual in particular, and in general for all priests and religious men, and for all the members of this confraternity, the spirit of steadiness and zeal in discharging the duties of their own state and office. He shall say three times : O, divine Heart, that dost truly love and adore the Almighty God, have mercy on us! His virtue is to consist in a profound respect, which he wil observe in church, by remaining there with great modesty and recollection of mind : because Jesus Christ is there in the most Holy Sacrament; and every day, five acts of this virtue shall be performed.

MAXIM :—That which is adored cannot truly be glorified unless it be imitated also.

ASPIRATION.

Oh, sweetest Heart of Jesus, I implore
That 1 may ever love thee, more and more.

PRAYER.

O, my Jesus, worthy adorer of the Divine Majesty, I join myself with my whole soul to the adorations which thou dost render to thy heavenly Father in the secrecy of thy Divine Heart; and I would wisch that all the faith and love with which thou inspirest the most Blessed Virgin Mary, and thy Saints, would be contained in mine, in order to honour and glorify thee now and forever, in proportion to thy merits. Amen.

Say the prayers to the Blessed Trinity and te the B. V. Mary, as before, pp. 207, 208.

FOURTH OFFICE.
LOVER.

THE Lover of the Sacred Heart of Jesus shall recompense it for the indifference and coldness of so many hearts which are consecrated to him. During the day, let him frequently join himself to the choir of Seraphims in exercising acts of love towards the most Holy Heart of Jesus, and pray those inflamed spirits, that during his repose during the night, they would supply his place before the most Holy Sacrament; which, therefore he shall, if possible, visit before he goes to bed, and leave his heart in the sacred tabernacle. In lying down on his bed, let him say : » I sleep, but my heart is watching with that of my beloved. » If he should wake during the night, he shall unite himself again with the heavenly lovers, whom he left in his place. In the prayer of the next morning, he shall return thanks to those angels, and renew the protest of his love towards the Sacred Heart, and earnestly beseech it to revive the flame of charity in so many cold and lukewarm hearts, that all may be ardent, and be at length consumed by the flames of his love. He shall repeat three times: O! most amiable Heart, grant that we may be inflamed with the fire of love for thee, now and forever. His virtue shall be the fidelity of the spouse mentioned in the Holy Canticles, who, through the ferfor of her very pure affections, charms the heart of her bridegroom : a great care, moreover, in everything, how small soever it may seem, for love's sake; and of this virtue, five acts shall be performed every day.

MAXIM : — No one can attain to the happiness of the divine love, unless he be aided by this divine love itself.

ASPIRATIONS.

Oh, sweetest Heart of Jesus, I implore
That I may ever love thee, more and more.

PRAYER.

O! MOST Holy Heart of Jesus, divine receptacle of that heavenly flame which thou camest to kindle upon the earth, and which thou so much desirest to be burning in all hearts; grant, I beseech thee, that our hearts may be consumed by such ardent flames. O! Angels of the heavenly court, I pray and conjure you that you would tell the Author of

my life that I am pining with an unceasing love for him. Amen.
Say the prayers to the Blessed Trinity, and to the B. V. Mary, as before, pp. 207, 208.

FIFTH OFFICE.
DISCIPLE.

The Disciple of the Heart of Jesus shall listen to it both in his prayers and meditations, and in receiving the most Holy Sacrament. He shall desire and implore that all men, and especially those who apply themselves to the teaching of others, would avail themselves of the doctrine of Jesus-Christ, and never resist him. During the day, he shall frequently enter into this Divine Heart as into a divine school, wherein the science of pure love is taught, which causes all worldly science to be forgotten. Let him repeat in his soul, the lessons which will be given him for his instruction; and let him join himself to the choir of the Cherubim, to share with them in the light and brightness which shine out of the Heart of Jesus. He shall moreover beseech this merciful Heart to spread its beams over so many followers of error, that they may embrace the truth; for this intention, the most Holy Sa-

216 SACRED HEART OF JESUS.

crament shall be visited, and the Veni Creator, &c., said. His virtues shall be recollection of mind, and silence, and every day let him make five acts of them.

MAXIM : — The more he will keep silence, the more learned will he become, and the better will he retain the interesting lessons of his adorable Teacher, viz. : Meekness, Humility. (Ven. Mary Marg.)

ASPIRATION.

O! mild Heart of my Jesus,
Grant I may love thee more and more.

PRAYER.

He very shortly will become learned whom thou, O, Divine Heart, undertakest to teach. Ah! teach me also, O! Amiable Heart! and since thou hast been so good as to admit me as thy Disciple, grant that my heart may be docile to thy divine lessons, and convert all those who are opposed to truth.

Say the prayers to the Blessed Trinity and to the B. V. Mary, as before, pp. 207, 208.

SIXTH OFFICE.

VICTIM.

THE Victim must consider himself as a sacrifice in order to appease God's wrath against sinners. During the day, he shall oftentimes present himself to the most Sacred Heart of Jesus, to partake of the state of a victim, as it is in the most Holy Sacrament; and in compliance with the motions of its earnest charity, shall say, « Amen. » With such a disposition he shall visit it at the sacred altar, upon which it was sacrificed by love, and falling prostrate upon the ground shall adore the divine Justice in union with the choir of Virtues. Let him sacrifice himself to this adorable Heart, as it sacrified itself; and let him present to the Eternal Father his sacrifice, together with that of the Heart of Jesus, especially during Mass and Communion, to obtain more easily the divine mercy for poor wretched sinners. He shall renew this spirit of sacrifice, particulary on Friday; and every day shall offer some virtuous action to the Sacred Heart of Jesus, with an act of consecration. His virtue is to be mortification, chiefly concerning curiosity of the mind, the affections of the heart and the gratification of the sences ; and he shall every day perform five acts of this virtue.

MAXIM. : — If it be the divine love that offers up the victim, how painful soever may be its strokes, they become agreable.

ASPIRATION.

O ! mild Heart of my Jesus,
Grand I may love thee more and more.

PRAYER.

O ! most Holy Heart, who upon our altars makest thyself a victim of love what else dost thou desire, what dost thou seek but victims, to continue in thy sacrifice ? Behold me here, O ! Lord ; lay hold on me, that I may be a victim sacrificed and consumed in the flames of thy love, for the greater glory of thy Eternal Father and for the salvation of sinners. Oh ! Heavenly Father, who hast chosen me as a victim, be pleased to accept me through the Sacred Heart of thy only Son, sacrificed for me. Amen.

Say the prayers to the Blessed Trinity and to the B. V. Mary, as before, pp. 207, 208,

SEVENTH OFFICE.

FAITHFUL SERVANT.

THE Faithful Servant of the Sacred Heart of Jesus shall place all his glory in bearing the bonds of the tender and generous love which keeps it a willing prisoner in the most Holy Sacrament. Therefore, every hour of the day he shall again and again offer up his obedience to the divine Heart of Jesus as to his Master and Lord, by saying. « O! Lord, I am thy servant; » and by prefering in everything the most holy will of the same to his own. Moreover, knowing that the great desire of Jesus Christ in the most holy Eucharist, is to impart himself to our souls trough holy communion, he shall beg of him whenever visited at the altar, that the offering he gives of all his good works, may be acceptable to him, in order that this adorable Sacrament may be received oftener and more worthily, and may produce in every heart the fruits of grace and salvation, of which it is calculated to be the spring. On this account, let him also engage the choir of Archangels in such a service of love, that they would call upon those who are invited to the Holy Table, and adorn them with the bridal dress. Finally, he shall say three times the *Our Father* & c.

MAXIM : — To serve the most Sacred Heart of Jesus, is to reign ; to live within it, is true happiness ; and to die therrein, is the ardent desire of a faithful soul. His virtue shall be faithfulness in obeying the divine inspirations ; and every day five acts of it shall be performed.

ASPIRATION.

Oh ! mild Heart of my Jesus !
Grant I may love thee, more and more.

PRAYER.

O ! OMNIPOTENT love of my God, who hast broken the chains that restrained me far from thee. Ah! would to God that I could persuade all those who wandered as I did, to taste at thy altars as I do, the delights of this new service which renders happy all those that embrace it. O! mysterious subjection of Jesus in the Sacrement of his love, I devote myself entirely to honour thee and to endeavor, or to desire at least, that every heart may be turned to thee. — Amen.

Say the prayers to the Blessed Trinity and to the B. V. Mary, as before, pp. 207, 208.

SACRED HEART OF JESUS.

EIGHTH OFFICE.

SUPPLIANT.

THE Implorer of the most Holy Heart of Jesus being penetraded with a lively faith and firm confidence in the merits of this divine Heart shall make an offering of them to the Eternal Father, in order to obtain His abundant graces for himself as well as for those who are in danger either of body or soul; but he shall chiefly pray for those who are in the agony of death, and for the suffering souls of Purgatory. For this reason, every hour of the day, and in the night too, when awake, let him accompany the tender and compassionate Heart of Jesus, and excite the remembrance of its inflamed charity. In his communions and prayers especially, he shall beg of God that his humble petition be heard benignly in behalf of his adorable Heart, the object with which he is pleased. Let him invite the choir of Angels, and chiefly the Guardian Angels, to accompany him in his visit to the most Holy Sacrament, during which he shall say the *Our Father*, and present all his good works for the above mentioned intention. His virtue shall be charity towards his neighbor, and humanity, and of them he shall perform five acts every day.

SACRED HEART OF JESUS.

MAXIM: — Through Jesus-Christ, every favor most holy Heart is open to all. Let us then enter into it with confidence, as into the divine sanctuary. Let us offer up our humble prayers in union with those of Jesus-Christ, and let us be assured they will not fail of being favorably received.

ASPIRATIONS.

O! mild Heart of my Jesus!
Grant I may love thee, more and more.

PRAYER.

O! DIVINE Heart! hear the cries of the needy, and be the consoler of the afflicted; since thou hast been always pleased, O! merciful Heart, to forgive, and to do good to all.

NINTH OFFICE.
ZEALOUS.

THE Zealous for the salvation of others, shall take a special care in procuring the glory of the Sacred Heart of Jesus, by promoting, above all, the perfection of his brethren. Let him invoke the nine choirs of angels, and chiefly that of the Principalities, that through their intercession this most Holy Heart of Jesus may be known every where throughout the earth : and that it would please the same to inspire with love for it so many Idolators and Gentiles, who do not know it, and so many Christians who refuse to pay it due homage. This must be the object he shall have in view in visiting the most Holy Sacrament, and during the thanksgiving after Communion. Moreover he shall, every hour of the day, glorify this adorable Heart by raising aloft his mind, in order to give satisfaction to its love, for the faults which may have been committed in the confraternity, and for those of his associates who may have negligently acquitted themselves of their allotted offices.

His virtues is to consist in understanding, with a holy zeal and prudence, to prevent as much as possible the outrages which might be offered to the Sacred Heart of Jesus, by procuring love for his adorable Heart by word and example. And to execute this more earnestly, let him be informed that our Lord has prepared incomprehensible treasures of grace for the zealous, and that his name is written in the Divine Heart, never to be erased (Ven. Mary Alac.)

MAXIM :—The Heart of Jesus breathed nothing but zeal for the glory of the Erernal Father, ant it requires of us to imitate him in doing the same. Where there is no zeal, says St, Austin, there is no love.

ASPIRATION.

O! mild Heart of my Jesus !
Grand I may love thee more and more.

PRAYER

O! SACRED Heart! who dost love us so fervently, how amiable art thou thyself! Ah! when will I see thee earnestly loved by all ! Oh! could I spread abroad the wonders of thy love, and obtain from every heart a correspondence to it.

AN ACT OF ATONEMENT
(EVERY FRIDAY.)
To the Sacred Heart of Jesus.

O! ADORABLE Heart of my Saviour and my God, penetrated with a lively sorrow at the sight of the outrages which Thou hast received, and which Thou daily dost receive in the Sacrament of Thy love, behold me prostrate at the foot of Thy altar, to make an acceptable atonement. O! that I were able, by my hommage and veneration, to make satisfaction to Thine injured honor, and efface with my tears and with my blood, so many irreverences, profanations, and sacrileges- which outrage thine infinite goodness. How well should my life be disposed of, could it be sacrificed for so worthy an object! Pardon, Divine Saviour, my ingratitude, and all the infidelities and indignities which I myself have committed against Thy Sovereign Majesty. Remember that Thy adorable Heart, bearing the weight of my sins in the days of its mortal life, was sorrowful even unto death; do not suffer Thy agony and Thy blood to be unprofitable to me. Annihilate whitin me my criminal heart, and give one according to thine—a heart contrite and humble, a heart pure and spotless, a heart which may be henceforth a victim consecrated to Thy glory, and inflamed with the sacred fire of Thy love. O! Lord, I deplore in the bitterness of my heart,, my former irreverences and sacrileges, which I wish in future to repair, by my pious deportment in the churches, my assiduity in visiting and my devotion and fervor in receiving the most holy Sacrament of the altar. But in order to render my respect and my adoration more grateful to Thee, I unite them wit those which are rendered to Thee in our temples, by those blessed spirits who are at the foot of Thy sacred tabernacles. Hear their vows, O! my God, and accept the homages of a heart which returns to thee with the sole view of loving only Thee, that may merit loving Thee eternally. Amen.

AN ACT OF CONSECRATION
(FOR THE FIRST FRIDAY OF THE MONTH.)

To the Adorable Heart of Jesus.

I give and consecrate to the Adorable Heart of Jesus my being, my life, my thoughts, my words, my actions, my pains, and my sufferings. I wish for life only, that my days may be employed in loving, honoring and adoring it. I thake Thee, then, O! Divine Heart, for the object of my love, the protector of my life, the assurance of my salvation, the remedy of my inconstancy, the repairer of all my defects, and my certain asylum at the hour of my death. O! Heart, abounding in mercy, turn from me the arrows of the just wrath of the Celestial Father. I place all my confidence in Thee; for I fear everything from my weakness, as I hope for everything from thy goodness.

Destroy in me everything which may displease and resist thee; implant so deeply Thy love in my heart that I may never forget Thee, nor be separated from Thee. I conjure Thee by Thy infinite goodness, to transform me into a victim entirely consecrated to Thy glory, which may be from this moment inflamed, and one day consumed in the fire of Thy love. This is the only object of my desires having no other ambition than that of living and dying in Thee and for Thee. Amen.

ORIGIN AND END
OF THE
SODALITY OF THE B. VIRGIN MARY.

The first Sodality of the Blessed Virgin, which was formed in Rome in 1563, owes its origin to the zealous exertions of Leo Lera, a Father of the Society of Jesus, who was then teaching in the Roman College. He collected youths and placed them under the special protection of the Blessed

Virgin. The pious and exemplary conduct of the first Sodalists caused associations of a similar nature to spread from Rome to every part of the Christian world.

In 1584 in an encyclical letter, Pope Gregory the XIII, approved the Sodality established in Rome, and extended to all the fathful the privilege of becoming members; he wished that the Sodality of the Roman College, under the title of the « *Annunciation of the Blessed Virgin Mary*, » should be, as it were the mother and centre of all the others: and he gave to the General of the Society of Jesus, all the necessary powers to direct these pious associations. Pope Sixtus V, Gregory XV, Clement VIII, Benedict XIV, Clement XIII, Pius VII, &c., have enriched the Sodality of the Blessed Virgin with indulgences, and extolled its utility in the warmest manner. Soon after its institution it numbered among its members, Popes, Cardinals, Bishops and many most zealous and learned clergymen, and likewise many secular Princes, Magistrates and men distinguished in every class of society. Among the Saints who have sanctified themselves by a faithful compliance with the rules of the Sodality, of which they were members, we might mention St. Charles Borromeo St. Francis of Sales, St. Aloysius, St. Stanislaus Kostka.

Advantages of the Sodality.

EXPERIENCE shows that Sodalities are a means of most abundant graces; for Sodalists are generally most faithful in the discharge of all the duties that the obligations Christianity impose. This extraordinary fidelity is to be attributed to the advantages they enjoy :

1. In the *special* protection which the B. Virgin extends to those who, in a special manner devote themselves to her; for she aids such in their necessities, consoles them in affliction, protects them in danger, supports them in their infirmities, strengthens them in their last moments and finally procures for them the grace of a holy and happy death.

2. In the zeal of a careful Director, who devotes his particular attention to their spiritual welfare, who instructs them in their duties and gives them wholesome advice when their salvation might be in danger.

3. In the numerous exhortations and pious discourses which renew their fervor and nourish their devotion, and which, by repeatedly

BLESSED VIRGIN MARY. 231

presenting to their minds the exalted character of the Blessed Virgin, encourage them to imitate her purity, meekness, patience and other virtues.

4. In their mutual good example, which is a powerful incentive to the practice of virtue.

5. In the prayers which they recite in common to which our Saviour promises a peculiar efficacy, for he says : « where two or three are united in my name, I am in the midst of them »

6. In the mutual succors of Christian charity. What was said of the first Christians may be applied to Sodalists : « *Of the multitude of believers there was one heart and one soul.* » In sickness, and in every affliction, they receive from their associates, all that relief and consolation which the most assiduous attention and ardent charity can bestow.

7. In the obligation they take opon themselves of observing the rules of the Sodality, of frequenting the Sacraments, of consenting to be admonished of their faults, even of taking in good part the slight penances imposed for their tepidity and negligence. These obligations, it is true, are non contracted under pain of sin, but they place a man of honor, a man faithful to his solemn promises, under the happy necessity of being virtuous.

8. In the merit of the good works performed by all the membres of the innumerable pious and charitable associations, wich afford pelief to all the ills to which mankind are subject. Such are the congregations whose object it is to ransom captives, to reconcile enemies ; to terminrte lawsuits, to relieve the poor, to instruct the ignorant, to visit the sick, etc., in the merits of which the members of the Sodality participate.

9. In the *Indulgences* which it is in their power to gain, and thus to cancel that vast amount of debt, the temporal punishment due to a multitude of sins, a release from which affords so great consolation to the Christian. The Saints always unterstood the value of the indulgences of the holy Church, and made corresponding exertions to obtain them. « *My son,* » said St. Louis, King of France, at the conclusion of his will, « *my son, remember to gain the inhulgences of the Holy Church.* » They are the following :

1. *Plenary Indulgences* granted to the Sodalists who, having received the Sacraments of penance and the holy Eucharist, shall say the usual prayers according to the intention of the Church :

1. On the day of reception.

2. On the day of the regular Assembly, or on the following day.

3. On the two principal festivals of the Sodality, or on the day to which they have been transferred.

4. On a communion day after a general Confession, once or twice a year.

5. On the festivals of the Nativity and Ascension of our Lord, and of the Annunciation, Immaculate, Conception, Nativity and Assumption of the Blessed Virgin Mary.

6. On a communion day in time of sickness having said three times, the *Our Fhater*, and *Hail Mary* before a Crucifix.

7. At the hour of death, by pronouncing devoutly (at least in the heart) the holy name of Jesus and Mary.

II. *Indulgences of Seven years* for each of the following works :

1. Attending the funeral of a Sodalist or any other Christian.

2. Praying fer dying or dead persons, viz : *Our Father,* and *Hail Mary*.

3. Attending Mass on week days.

4. Examination of conscience before going to bed.

5. Visiting the sick, or those who are in prison.

6. Reconciling enemies.

7. Attending a public or private meeting of piety, a sermon or spiritual instruction.

Observations.

1. All the preceding indulgences are applicable to the sols in Purgatory.
2. The altar of the Sodality is privileged for deceased Sodalists ontly.
3. Sodalists in any part of the world may gain all these and the following Indulgences, either in the church of the place in which they reside, or elsewhere as circumstances may permit.

III. *Indulgences of the Stations.* Many of them are very considerable, and can be gained at Rome, by visiting certain privileged churches; but they are also granted to members who, on a station day, visit the church or chapel of the Sodality, or of the place where they reside, and say seven times, the *Our Father,* and *Hail Mary.*

The principal Station days are the following: —The festivals of the Circumcision and Epiphany, the three Sundays, Septuagesima, Sexagesima and Quinquagesima. On every day of Lent, on Easter Sunday, and each day of the Octave; also on the feast of St. Mark and on Rogation-days. On the Ascension of Christ, the Eve of Pentecost, Pentecost with each day of its Octave. On Ember days and the four Sundays of Advent. On the Eve of Christmas; on Christmas and the three following days. (See Bouvier.)

10. All those who have once made their act of consecration remain membres of the Sodality and participate in all its advantages, even after having left the place where the Sodality exists, provided they observe the rules, as well as the circumstances of the time and place may permit.

Compendium of the General Rules of the Sodality.

1. THE Sodality shall be governed by one of the Fathers of the Society of Jesus, who is called its *Director*, by a Prefect with two Assistants, a Secretary, and six Consultors (or more as the Father may direct,) to be chosen from among the membres of the Sodality, twice a year, or oftener, at the Director's discretion All must ondeavor not only to respect and to obey their Father Director, but also the other officers, in whatever concerns their respective duties in the Sodality.

2. Every one must be solicitous that his

regular mode of conduct, irreprehensible manners ans virtuous conversations, reflect honor on the Sodality and the Blessed Virgin, Patroness and Mother, of whom he professes himself an adopted child, mindful of his solemn promise; *Never to say or do anything against her honor.* »

3. As the end of tnis association is the practice of true virtue and piety, and progress in learning, whoever wishes to be received into it, must make a general confession of his past life (unless his confessor should think otherwise.) Moreover, on the first Sunday of every month the Sodalists shall approach the Sacraments of confession and communion, but the Officers somewhat oftener, as it is their particular duty to excel their companions in true piety. The Nativity of our Lord, the Circumcision, Resurrection and Ascension, Pentecost and Corpus Christi, the Immaculate Conception, Annunciation and Assumption of our Blessed Lady, and the Feast of All Saints, are appointed days of Communion for all.

With regard to Confession, it is of the greatest importance, and it is hereby recommended to all the members, to have their fixed and permanent Confessor, as far as may be in different circumstances practicable.

4. On sundays and appointed festivals, all shall assemble in the Oratory for spiritual exercises, which will be conducted by the Director, and to which no one shall be admitted who is not a member, without leave of the Director. At the opening of each meeting, shall be said by the Prefect, the hymn « Veni Creator Spiritus, » with the verse and prayer, and at the close the appropriate antiphon of the Blessed Virgin, which the Church uses at the end of the divine Office.

5. The members shall hear Mass everyday but when they have received the holy Communion, they shall spend at least a quarter of an hour in thanksgiving.

6. Every morning, when they rise, they shall recite three times, *Our Father* and *Hail Mary*, in honor of the Holy Trinity, once the *Apostles Creed*, and « *Hail Holy Queen,* » besides other prayers which devotion may suggest. At night they shall make an examination of conscience, and say the *Our Father* and *Hail Mary*, three times, and once the Psalm, « *de Profundis*, » for the souls of the faithful departed.

7. Since the Sodalists make greater profession of christian perfection than others they should also endeavor to perform more works of charity, mercy, piety and devotion.

8. All should love one another with mutual

charity, and endeavor to make daily progress in true virtue. They should therefore seek the company of the good, and with the greatest care avoid communications with the evil and all occasions of sin, such as quarrels, contentions and unbecoming sports, that every one may perceive that they are worthy clients of the Blessed Virgin.

9. They must guard themselves in a special manner against idleness, the fatal origin of so many, nay of all vices; they must consequently perform their respective daily duties with attention and diligence.

10. Should any one be absent from the ordinary meetings, he shall assign the reason for his absence to the Director. On account of frequent absense, or other faults, any one may be suspended for a time, or dismissed from the Sodality, in order to conserve in its members the spirit of fervor and regularity.

11. When any of the Sodalists falls sick, the Director will take care to send some one or two to visit him, and will strengthen him with the holy Sacraments, and all will recommend him in their prayers. Should he be called to a better life, all shall recite once, either in common or privately, the office of the dead, and for the eight succeeding days they shall hear

BLESSED VIRGIN MARY. 239

Mass and say the Psalm « *De profundis,* » or the repose of his soul.

12. Postulants will be subjected to a trial for one month, or longer, at the expiration of which time the Director may admit them as members, provided they have given satisfactory proofs of their piety and made their first communion.

13. That these rules may be more easily observed, not only shall each one have and read them often, but they shall also be publicly read at certain times appointed by the Director.

Office of the Immaculate Conception of the Blessed Virgin Mary.

At Matins.

V. Come, Oh my voice, and let us raise.
R. To heaven's bright queen a song of praise.
V. Propitious thought, Oh Mother send us,
R. And from the dreadful foe defend us.
V. Glory be to the Father, &c.

OFFICE OF THE

Hail, mistress of earth; hail heavenly queen.
Hail, Virgin of Virgins! all chaste and serene!
Bright star of the morning! the light of whose face
Reflects His effulgence, who filled thee with grace.
Oh, sovereign of Angels! come quickly we pray,
And drive every ill, that besets us, away.

  Thee from Eternity
  God did ordain,
  Over his household
  As mistress to reign;
  Thee he predestined
  The Mother to be
  Of him who created
  Earth, Heaven and Sea
  Thee he elected
  The Spouse of his heart,
  Because in our sin
  Thou never had'st part.

V. God elected and prepared her,
R. And gave his own Tabernacle for a dwelling.

  Let us Pray.
Oh Holy Mary! Mother of our Lord

IMMACULATE CONCEPTION. 241

Jesus Christ, Queen of Heaven and Mistress of the World! who never forsakest nor despisest any one, look upon us with an eye of pity, and beg of thy beloved Son the pardon of all our sins, that we who now devoutly celebrate the Immaculate Conception, may receive the reward of eternal joy, through the mercy of Jesus Christ our Lord, whom thou, pure Virgin, did'st bring into the world, and who, with the Father and the Holy Ghost in perfect Trinity, liveth and reigneth One God, world without end. AMEN.

V. O Mother, turn a mother's ear,
R. And kindly our petitions hear.
V. Blessed be our Lord.
R. Thanks be to God.
V. May the souls of the faithful departed, through the mercy of God, rest in peace.
R. Amen.

At Prime.

V. Thy help, propitious Mother, lend us,
R. And from the dreadful foe defend us.

V. Glory be to the Father, &c.

Hail, virginal wisdom, hail, mansion of God,
Where seven-fold pillars befit his abode!
All stately without and all perfect within,
He chose him a dwelling undarkened by sin;
For even before thy miraculous birth,
Thou wert free from the stain that has sullied the earth.

Mother of all saints,
Living and dead,
New star that shone
Over Israels head;
Sovereign of Angels,
Terror of hell,
Be our refuge,
Who love thee so well.

V. In His Holy Spirit He created her;
R. And exalted her above all his works.

Let us pray. — Oh, Holy Mary, &c.

At Tierce..

V. Thy help, propitious Mother, lend us
R. And from the dreadful foe defend us.
V. Glory be to the Father, &c.

Hail, Ark of the Covenant! Solomon's throne,
The Rainbow thou art, thro' the Deluge that shone.
Bright Bush of the Vision! fair flowering Rod!
Sweet Morsel of Samson; sealed Closet of God!

  Oh how befitting
  The wisdom Divine,
  To prepare for Himself
  A Nature like thine,
  To which not a speck
  Of the error of Eve,
  That taints all beside,
  For a moment could cleave.

V. My dwelling-place is in the highest heavens;
R. And my throne I have placed above the clouds.

Let us pray. — Oh, Holy Mary, &c.

At Sixth.

V. Thy help, propitious Mother, lend us.
R. And from the dreadful foe defend us.

V. Glory be to the Father, &c.

Hail, Virginal Mother! hail, Temple Divine
The glory of Angels, and Purity's shrine;
Hail, comfort of mourners, bright garden of joy,
Whose beauties the songs of all Angels employ—
The type of thy patience is Victory's palm—
Thy Chastity's figure, the fragrance of Balm.

> Oh blessed the clay
> Out of which thou wert wrought,
> And utterly free
> From original blot;
> Oh, city exhalted,
> Bright orient gate,
> What graces unite
> In thy singular state!

V. Like to a lily in the midst of thorns,
R. So among Adam's daughters is my beloved.

Let us pray. Oh, Holy Mary, etc.

At None.

V. Thy help, propitious Mother, lend us,
R. And from the dreadful foe defend us.
V. Glory be to the Father, &c.

IMMACULATE CONCEPTION.

Hail, city of Refuge, the safety of all ;
Hail, Tower of David, Impregnable wall ;
All flaming with zeal for man in his woe,
Throu crushest the head of his Stygian foe.
      Invincible woman,
      Than Judith more bold,
      Or Abigail, cherishing
      David of old ;—
      Rachel a Saviour
      To one people gave—
      Thou a Redeemer,
      All nations to save.

V. All fair art thou, my beloved !
R. And there was never stain of Adam's sin in thee !

Let us pray.—Oh, Holy Mary, etc.

At Even-Song.

V. Thy help, propitious Mother, lend us,
R. And from the dreadful foe defend us.
V. Glory be to the Father, &c.

Hail, wonderful dial, Ezechias of old
  Beheld, when the prophet his destiny told ;
The word that incarnate in thee, did become,
  Receded—descending to man's lowly home :

OFFICE OF THE

Nine choirs he passed of superior powers,
To take up the tenth in this nature of ours.

 The beams of this sun
 Are the light of thy face;
 And thou the Aurora
 Preceding his race:
 The serpent that lurks
 In night's desperate gloom,
 Thou crushest and causest
 All beauties to bloom.

V. I have caused a never failling light to rise in Heaven;
R. And like a luminous veil, have spread it over all the earth.

Let us pray.—Oh, Holy Mary, etc.

At Compline.

V. May Jesus Christ, thy Son, at thy intercession, convert us,
R. And turn away his anger from us forever.
V. Thy help, propitious Mother, lend us,
R. And from the dreadful foe defend us.
V. Glory be to the Father, &c.

IMMACULATE CONCEPTION. 247

Hail, Virgin productive, yet Mother unstain'd.
A Virgin brought forth, yet a Virgin remained!
No crown was e're given to creature, like thine,—
Twelve stars are the gems in its circle that shine.
Above all the Angels—immaculate – pure—
At the right of the King, thou shalt sit evermore.

   Oh Mother, through thee,
   The sinner's great hope—
   Bright star of the sea!—
   May Paradise ope;—
   And thee, in thee mansions
   Of peace and of rest,
   With the sight of thy Son
   May our vision be blessed.

V. Like fluent oil, Oh Mary is thy name;
R. And thy servants have loved thee.
Oh how much!

Let us Pray.—Oh, Holy Mary, &c.

   Sweet Virgin, we offer
   On suppliant knee,
   These prayers that the Church
   Has devoted to thee!
   Oh Mary conduct us
   In happiness' way;

248 OFFICE OF THE IMMACUL. CONCEPTION.

And at the last hour
Assist us, we pray. AMEN.

Anthem.

100 DAYS INDULGENCE BY PAUL V.

There is a bough in which no blur of either kind,
Original, or wrought hath touched the virgin rind.

V. In thy conception, O Virgin, thou wert immaculate.

R. Pray for us to the Father, whose Son thou didst bear.

PRAYER.

Oh God, who by the immaculate conception of the blessed Virgin Mary didst prepare a worthy habitation for thy Son, we beseech thee, that as by the foresight of his death, thou didst exempt her from all stain, so we, purified by her intercession, may come to thee, through the same Jesus Christ our Lord, whom with Thee and the Holy Ghost, &c. AMEN.

Prayers used in the Sodality.

FORMULA OF ADMISSION.

HOLY MARY, immaculate Virgin, Mother

of God, I,_____ chose thee, this day, for my mother, queen, patroness and advocate; and I firmly resolve never to depart, either in word or deed, from the duty which I owe to thee, nor suffer those who are committed to my charge to say or do anything against thy honour and the respect thou deservest. Receive me, therefore, as thy devoted servant forever; assist me in all the actions of my life, and forsake me not at the hour of my death. Amen.

FORMULA FOR THE ADMISSION AS CANDIDATES.

Holy Mary, immaculate Virgin, Mother, of God, I, _____ anxious to become one of thy privileged children, resolve, on this day, with the divine assistance and aided by thy powerful intercession, to amend my life and imitate thy virtues, so as to deserve to be received as a member of this holy Sodality erected to thy honour, and to the greater glory of thy divine Son. Amen.

𝔓𝔯𝔞𝔶𝔢𝔯𝔰 𝔭𝔯𝔢𝔰𝔠𝔯𝔦𝔟𝔢𝔡 𝔦𝔫 𝔱𝔥𝔢 𝔰𝔦𝔵𝔱𝔥 𝔘𝔲𝔩𝔢 𝔣𝔬𝔯 𝔢𝔳𝔢𝔯𝔶 𝔡𝔞𝔶.

IN THE MORNING

THREE times *Our Father*, and *Hail Mary*, once the *Apostles' Creed*, and *Hail Holy Queen*, as before, pp. 35, 44.

IN THE EVENING

After the examination of conscience; three times *Our Father* and *Hail Mary*, and once the Psalm « *De profundis*, » as before, pp. 35, 69.

𝔓𝔯𝔞𝔶𝔢𝔯𝔰 𝔱𝔬 𝔭𝔯𝔢𝔰𝔢𝔯𝔳𝔢 𝔥𝔬𝔩𝔶 𝔓𝔲𝔯𝔦𝔱𝔶.

THROUGH thy sacred virginity and immaculate conception, obtain for me, O purest Virgin, purity, of soul and body.

PRAYER OFTEN RECITED BY THE HOLY SODALIST, ST. ALOYSIUS OF GONZAGUA.

O HOLY MARY! my Mother and Advocate, o thy care and particular protection, and into the bosom of thy mercy to-day and every day, and at the hour of my death, I commend my soul and body; all my hope and consolation, my difficulties and afflictions, my life, and the end of my life, I commend to thee; that, trough thy most powerful intercession, and through thy merits, all my words and actions may be directed according to thy will, and that of thy divine Son.

Prayer after Holy Communion.

BEHOLD me, o good and amiable Jesus, prostrate in thy Divine presence, and beseeching thee, with all the ardor of my soul, to impress upon my heart lively sentiments of faith, hope, and charity, and repentance for my sins, and a most determined resolution of never offending thee again; whilst with all the affection of my heart, and with the sincerest sorrow, I consider and contemplate thy five wounds, meditating chiefly on the words of the

Royal Prophet concerning thee, O my Jesus!—« They have pierced my hands and feet; they have numbered all my bones. »

OBSERVATION.—A Plenary Indulgence is granted to all the faithful who devoutly recite this prayer before an image of Christ crucified, provided they go to Confession and Communion, and that they pray for some time according to the intention of His Holiness. It is also applicable to the souls in Purgatory.

ASSOCIATION OF THE HOLY INFANCY.

Formed principally for children under the age of twelve years but admirably suited for persons of all ages.

The Society of the Holy Infancy is chiefly formed for young children;—hence they have the first rank or place of honor nearest the Holy Child Jesus. It is a favor, a special grace when they become members of it while very young. These tender nurslings of the flock of Jesus Christ have the greatest share in the public prayers of the Association, and in all the Masses celebrated in the principal sanctuaries

THE HOLY INFANCY. 253

consecrated to the Holy Infancy of Jesus and to the most Holy Virgin.

SECOND CLASS OR GRADE OF ASSOCIATES.

But besides this first class of associates, the Society has a second, composed of persons of every age. The age of twelve years is the sacred limit which separates the first grade from the second; but both classes of membres really participate in the prayers, spiritual favors, merits, and indulgences in all cases annexed to membership and fulfilment of conditions.

DUTIES OF EVERY MEMBER.

1. To pay punctually a monthly subscription of one cent, or *twelve* cents for the year, in advance.

2. To recite every day one Hail Mary, and the aspiration, *Mary and Joseph, pray for us, and for all poor heathen children.* (If the child is too young to say these prayers, another associate can say them for it.)

3. Every child must receive once for all, on entering the Association, a picture or medal as a pledge of membership.

Rules for the First Class of Members.

1. Every little child so favored as to belong to the Holy Infancy, should show, as a special mark of gratitude and love, a tender devotion to the holy Infant Jesus. Every morning she should go on her knees and beg his blessing, bowing her head to receive it.

2. Whenever they hear the Holy Name of Jesus, they will bow their heads in token of their respect.

3. They must try to be as obedient as the Holy Child Jesus was, to be as truthful as he was, as innocent as he was in their words and actions. They must offer their little hands to Jesus, their little hearts to Jesus, their eyes

to Jesus, their ears, all their senses to him, and beg the Holy Child to keep their souls holy and pure.

4. They must endeavor to grow better every day of their lives and to so deport themselves that any one, on seeing them, may say : Oh! these are children who try to act as the Holy Child Jesus would act if he were here!

5. They must try and love the Blessed Mother and dear St. Joseph as the Holy Child did. They must often say a little prayer to their Guardian Angels, repeating : Dear Angel Guardian, teach me to love the Holy Child Jesus!—or,

 « Angel of God, my Guardian dear,
 To whom his love commits me here,
 Ever this day be at my side
 To light and guard, to rule and guide. »
                                        Amen.

One hundred days indulgence every time for this aspiration.

INDULGENCES GRANTED TO THE HOLY CHILDHOOD.

I.—*Plenary Indulgences.*

1. From Christmas till the Presentation of Our Lord in the Temple.
2. From the second Sunday after Easter till the end of the month of May.

N. B. — This indulgence is applicable to the souls in Purgatory, and can be gained by assisting at a Mass said for the institute; it can also be gained by children who have not yet made their first communion.

3. Also on the patronal feasts of the institute, the Presentation, the Holy Guardian, Angels, St. Joseph, St. Francis Xaxier, and St. Vincent de Paul, on condition of praying for the incrase of the Holy Childhood.
4. On the anniversary of the baptism of the associates, and also bij their father,

mother, brothers, and sisters. (Applicable to the souls in Purgatory.)

II.—*Partial indulgences.*

1. Indulgence of seven years to all the associates who on the feasts of the Institution receive solemn benediction, given according to the particular form.

N. B.—These indulgences can be changed by the Bishops, and with their consent by the Directors of the work, to other more favorable times.

2. Indulgence of a year to the members of the committee of the Institution for each re-union at which they assist.

3. Indulgence of forty days for the associates and promoters of the work.

Each time that by word or action they augment, favor, or defend the pious association, and by it procure love of the Infant Jesus, and the salvation of souls.

258 ASSOCIATION OF THE HOLY INFANCY.

PRIVILEGES GRANTED TO THE DIRECTORS OF THE ASSOCIATION.

Faculty for five years, with the consent of the ordinary, to bless medals, beads, and statues of the Infant Jesus, as also medals, beads, and statues of the Virgin Mary, with the application of the ordinary indulgence, and even those of St. Bridget.

SPIRITUAL ADVANTAGES.

I. Each month two Masses in one of the twelve sanctuaries dedicated to Mary, or to the Holy Infancy of our Lord, celebrated for the intention of the associated, especially of those who have not yet made their first communion, and of Christian mothers to obtain for them that all their children may live to receive the grace of baptism.

II. Two Masses yearly for the associates, living or dead.

WARNING TO CHILDREN.

ONE of the most wicked and miserable parents that perhaps ever lived, had a son who was as bad as himself. Sunk in every kind of vice, they both plunged deeper and deeper into the abyss of destruction. The son was disobedient, wilful, passionate, and violent, even to fury. They were always disputing and quarrelling, and lived in continual strife. Each cursed the other. One day, when the father rebuked the son, and reproached him with his bad behavior, the wretched child seized his father, who was already advanced in years, and in a rage threw him on the ground and dragged him by the hairs of his head down the stairs, that he might throw him out of the house. When he had dragged him a little way, the father raised his voice and cried: Stop! wretch! when I was of your age I never dragged my father further than this! Thus, ad last, the sinful father acknowledged the justice of God, who permitted his son to treat him as he himself had treated his own father.

O how terrible are the judgments of God, but also how guilty are you, ye disobedient and unnatural children! Learn to respect your parents always, even when you see them to be wicked. I know that excesses so dreadful as what I have related are not of every-day occurence, but still I know that great disorders happen every day, not only among people of low condition, of coarse sentiments, and without education, but also among the rich and refined; not always perhaps so publicly manifest to the eyes of men, but well known to God, and detestable in his sight.

WARNING TO CHILDREN.

O, then, children, be always kind and affectionate, respectful and obedient to your parents. Try in every possible way to make them comfortable and happy, and to repay them for the many cares and anxieties they have suffered for you. This is the will of God, and he will recompense you for it. Hear what a splendid promise is attached to the commendment which he gives you: « *Honor thy father and thy mother, that thou mayest be long-lived upon the land which the Lord thy God will give thee.* »

Advice of St. Philip Neri to his Spiritual Children.

1. BLESSED are you, my children, who have time to do good.

2. Now is not the time for sleep; for Paradise was not made for cowards.

3. Children, keep up a scheerful temper. I will have no scruples or melancholy : only avoid sin.

4. Avoid inordinate mirth, becauce this roots up the little good which has been aquired.

5. You must not leave your devout exercises; but if you wish to recreate yourselves with a walk, let these be fulfilled, and then go.

6. Do not care to attempt to many devotions; but undertake a few, and persevere in them.

7, You must not look to becoming saints in four days, because perfection is acquired with great labor, and by degrees.

8. Do not have a fancy to be masters of spiritual matters and convert others, but attend to regulating yourself.

9. Children, mortify yourselves in small things, that you may afterwards be able the more easily to mortify yourselves in great things.

10. To choose your vocation, time is required, advice, and prayer.

11. To preserve chastity, it is an excellent prescription to discover your thoughts immediately to your confessor.

12. Do not nourish your body delicately, fly bad companions and evil communication.

13. Avoid idleness, especially during the hours after dinner; because it is at that time that the devil commonly makes his fiercest attacks.

14. Do not touch each other familiarly, not even in jest; nor have private conversations with each other.

15. Have no familiarity with women, although they may be allied to you by relationship.

16. Do not trust yourselves whatever may be your experience, but fly every occasion.

17. Go often to confession, at least every eight days; and go to communion according to the advice of your confessor.

18. Be devout to Mary, because this is the best means of obtaining the grace of God.

19. Before choosing a confessor, recommend yourselves in prayer to God; but having once chosen, do not readily change without just cause.

20. When at confession, tell your worst sins first, that the devil may not tempt you to end by hiding them.

21. Take counsel always of your spiritual father, and recommend yourselves to the prayers of all.

22. Give yourselves always, and in all things, into the hands of your superiors; because obedience is a compendious way to acquire perfection.

23. Pray continually to the Lord, that He may grant you the gift of perseverance.

24. Endeavor to have God always before your eyes.

25. Never excuse yourselves when corrected; and keep yourselves from saying any thing in your own praise, even in jest.

26. Read, O my children, the lives of the Saints; hear sermons; and do not fail to practise the prayers and other exercises of the con-

gregation; because they are very pleasing to the Divine majesty.

Children, in order not to fall into sin, keep profoundly engraved in your memories the three warnings given by a holy hermit to certain youths, and act according to them faithfully.

1st Warning. Fly the occasions of sin.
2d Warning. Fly the occasions of sin.
3d Warning. Fly the occasions of sin.
Fly quickly, fly far, fly always.

Children, do you really desire to be saved! Then ever keep,

First, eternity in mind ;
Secondly, God in your heart ;
Thirdly, the world under your lee.
« This do, and thou shalt live. » *

* Luke x 28

LITANY OF THE SAINTS.

Anthem. REMEMBER not, O Lord, our offences, nor those of our fathers; neither take thou vengeance of our sins.
Lord have mercy.
Lord have mercy.
Christ have mercy.
Christ have mercy.
Lord have mercy.
Lord have mercy.
Christ hear us.
Christ graciously hear us.
God the Father of heaven, *Have mercy on us.*
God the Son, Redeemer of the world, *Have mercy on us.*
God the Holy Ghost, *Have mercy on us.*
Holy Trinity, one God,
Holy Mary,
Holy Mother of God,
Holy Virgin of virgins,
St. Michael,
St. Gabriel,
St. Raphael,
All ye holy Angels and Archangels,
All ye holy orders of blessed Spirits,
St. John Baptist,
St. Joseph,
All ye holy Patriarchs and Prophets,

Pray for us.

St. Peter,
St. Paul,
St. Andrew,
St. James,
St. John,
St. Thomas,
St. James,
St. Philip,
St. Bartholomew,
St. Matthew,
St. Simon,
St. Thaddeus,
St. Matthias,
St. Barnabas,
St. Luke,
St. Mark,
All ye holy Apostles and Evangelistes,
All ye holy Disciples of our Lord,
All ye holy Innocents,
St. Stephen,
St. Lawrence,
St. Vincent,
SS. Fabian and Sebastian,
SS. John and Paul,
SS. Cosmas and Damian,
SS. Gervase and Protase,
All ye holy Martyrs,
St. Sylvester,
St. Gregory,
St. Ambrose,

Pray for us.

LITANY OF THE SAINTS.

St. Augustine,
St. Jerome,
St. Martin,
St. Nicholas,
All ye holy Bishops and Confessors,
All ye holy Doctors,
St. Anthony,
St. Benedict,
St. Bernard,
St. Dominic,
St. Francis,
All ye holy Priests and Levites,
All ye holy Monks and Hermits,
St. Mary Magdelene,
St. Agatha,
St. Lucy,
St. Agnes,
St. Cicily,
St. Catherine,
St. Anastasia,
All ye holy Virgins and Widows,
All ye holy men and women, Saints of God,

Pray for us.

Make intercession for us.
Be merciful,
Spare us, O Lord.
Be merciful,
Graciously hear us, O Lord.
From all evil, *O Lord, deliver us.*
From all sin, *O Lord, deliver us.*

LITANY OF THE SAINTS.

From thy wrath, *
From sudden and unlooked for death,
From the snares of the devil,
From anger, and hatred and every evil will,
From the spirit of fornication,
From lightning and tempest,
From everlasting death,
Through the mystery of thy holy Incarnation,
Through thy Coming,
Through thy Nativity,
Through thy Baptism and Holy Fasting,
Through thy Cross and Passion,
Through thy Death and Burial,
Through thy Holy Resurrection,
Through thine admirable Ascension,
Through the coming of the Holy Ghost the Paraclete,
In the day of judgment,
We sinners,
Beseech thee, hear us.
That thou wouldst spare us,
That thou wouldst pardon us,
That thou wouldst bring us to true penance,
That thou wouldst vouchsafe to govern and preserve thy holy Church,

O Lord, deliver us.

We beseech, &c.

---

* Here, for the Devotion of the Forty Hours, is inserted :

From all dangers that threaten us,
From plague, famine and war,

LITANY OF THE SAINTS.

That thou wouldst vouchsafe to preserve our Apostolic Prelate, and all orders of the Church,

That thou wouldst vouchsafe to humble the enemies of holy Church, *

That thou wouldst vouchsafe to give peace and true concord to Christian kings and princes,

That thou wouldst vouchsafe to grant peace and unity to all Christian people,

That thou wouldst vouchsafe to confirm and preserve us in thy holy service,

That thou wouldst lift up our minds to heavenly desires,

That thou wouldst render eternal blessings to all our benefactors,

That thou wouldst deliver our souls and the souls of our brethen, relations, and benefactors, from eternal damnation,

That thou wouldst vouchsafe to give and preserve the fruits of the earth,

That thou wouldst vouchsafe to grant eternal rest to all the faithful departed,

That thou wouldst vouchsafe graciously to hear us,

Son of God,

We beseech thee, hear us.

---

* For the Devotion of the Forty Hours, insert :

That thou wouldst vouchsafe to defeat the attempts of all Turks and heretics, and bring them to nought.

LITANY OF THE SAINTS.

Lamb of God who takest away the sins of the world, *Spare us, O Lord.*

Lamb of God who takest away the sins of the world,

Graciously hear us, O Lord.

Lamb of God, who takest away the sins of the world,

Have mercy on us.

Christ hear us.

Christ graciously hear us.

Lord have mercy.

Christ have mercy.

Lord have mercy.

Our Father (*secretly.*)

V. And lead us not into temptation.

R. But deliver us from evil.

Psalm lxix. *Deus in adjutorium.*

1. O God, come to my assistance : O Lord make haste to help me.

2. Let them be confounded and ashamed : that seek after my soul.

3. Let them be turned backward, and blush for shame : that desire evils unto me.

4. Let them be straightway turned backward blushing for shame, that say unto me : 'T is well, 't is well.

5. Let all that seek thee be joyful and glad in thee : and let such as love thy salvation say alway, The Lord be magnified.

6. But I am needy and poor : o God, help thou me.

7. Thou art my helper and my deliverer: O Lord, make no long delay.

Glory be, &c.

V. Save thy servants.

R. Who hope in thee, O my God.

V. Be unto us. O Lord, a tower of strength.

R. From the face of the enemy.

V. Let not the enemy prevail against us.

R. Nor the son of iniquity approach to hurt us.

V. O Lord, deal not with us according to our sins.

R. Neither requite us according to our iniquities.

V. Let us pray for our Sovereign Pontiff, N.

R. The Lord preserve him and give him life, and make him blessed upon the earth; and deliver him not up to the will of his ennemies.

V. Let us pray for our benefactors.

R. Vouchsafe, O Lord, for thy name's sake, to reward with eternall life all them that do us good. Amen.

V. Let us pray for the faithful departed.

R. Eternal rest give unto them, O Lord; and let perpetual light shine upon them.

V. Let them rest in peace. *R.* Amen.

V. For our absent brethren.

R. Save thy servants, who hope in thee, O my God.

V. Send them help, O Lord, from the sanctuary.

R. And defend them out of Sion.

LITANY OF THE SAINTS. 273

V. O Lord, hear my prayer.
R. And let my cry come unto thee.

*Let us Pray.**

O God, whose property is always to have mercy and to spare, receive our humble petition: that we, and all thy servants who are bound by the chain of sins, may, by the compassion of thy goodness, mercifully be absolved.

Graciously hear, we beseech thee, O Lord, the prayers of thy suppliants and forgive the sins of them that confess to thee; that, in thy bounty, thou mayest grant us both pardon and peace.

---

* For the Devotion of the Forty Hours the Following Collects are used:

O God, who, under a wonderful Sacrament, hast left us a memorial of thy Passion; grant us, we beseech thee, so to venerate the sacred mysteries of thy Body and Blood, that we may ever feel within us the fruit of thy redemption. Who livest, &c. Amen.

FROM ADVENT TO CHRISTMAS.

O God, who wast pleased that thy Word, at the message of an angel, should take flesh in the womb of the blessed Virgin Mary; grant to us, thy humble servants, that we who believe her to be truly the Mother of God, may be assisted by her intercessions with thee. Through the same Christ our Lord.
R. Amen.

Show forth upon us, O Lord, in thy mercy, thy unspeakable loving kindness; that thou mayest both loose us from all our sins, and deliver us from the punishments which we deserve for them.

O God, who by sin art offended, and by penance pacified, mercifully regard the prayers of thy people making supplication to thee, and turn away the scourges of thine anger, which we deserve for our sins.

Almighty, everlasting God, have mercy upon thy servant N , our Sovereign Pontiff, and direct him, according to thy clemency, into the way of everlasting salvation; that by thy grace he may both desire those things that are pleasing to thee, and perform them with all his strength.

O God, from whom all holy desires, all right counsels, and all just works do come, give unto thy servants that peace which the world cannot

FROM CHRISTMAS TO THE PURIFICATION.

O God, who, by the fruitful virginity of blessed Mary, hast given to mankind the rewards of eternal salvation; grant, we beseech thee, that we may experience her intercession for us, through whom we have merited to receive the author of life, our lord Jesus thy Son. Who liveth and reigneth with thee in the unity of the Holy Ghost, God, world without end.

R. Amen.

LITANY OF THE SAINTS. 275

give; that our hearts being devoted to thy commandments, and the fear of our enemies being taken away, our times, by thy protection, may be peaceful.

Inflame, O Lord, our reins and heart with the fire of the Holy Ghost; that we may serve thee with a chaste body, and please thee with a clean heart.

O God, the Creator and Redeemer of all the faithful, give to the souls of thy servants departed the remission of all their sins; that through pious supplications they may obtain the pardon which they have always desired.

FROM THE PURIFICATION TO ADVENT.

Grant, we beseech thee, O Lord God, that we, thy servants, may enjoy perpetual health of mind and body; and by the intercession of the blessed Mary ever Virgin, may be delivered from present sorrow, and attain eternal gladness.

THEN FOLLOWS THE COLLECT FOR THE POPE, AFTER WHICH IS SAID :

O God, our refuge and strength, who art the author of all piety, hearken unto the devout prayers of thy Church ; and grant that what we ask faithfully we may obtain effectually.

Almigthy, everlasting God, in whose hand are all the powers and all the rights of king-

LITANY OF THE SAINTS.

Prevent, we beseech thee, O Lord, our actions by thy inspirations, and further them with thy continual help; that every prayer and work of ours may always begin from thee, and through thee be likewise ended.

Almighty, everlasting God, who hast dominion over te living and the dead, and art merciful to all who thou foreknowest will be thine by faith and works; we humbly beseech thee that they for whom we intend to pour forth our prayers, whether this present world still detain them in the flesh, or the world to come hath already received them stripped of their mortal bodies, may, by the grace of thy loving kindness, and by the intercession of all the Saints, obtain the remission of all their sins Through thy Son Jesus-Christ our Lord, who liveth and reigneth with thee in the unity of the Holy Spirit, God, for ever and ever. R. Amen.

---

doms, come to the assistance of thy Christian people, that all pagan and heretical nations, who trust in their own violence and fraud, may be broken by the might of thy right hand.

Thew follows the last Collect, Omnipotens, sempiterne, Deus, &c., Almighty, everlasting God, &c , *with the Versicles. except that, in the last response but one, &c., instead of the simple* Amen, *is said,*

R. And ever preserve us. Amen.

V. O Lord, hear my prayer.
R. And let my cry come unto thee.
V. May the almighty and merciful Lord graciously hear us.
R. Amen.
V. And may the souls of the faithful, through the mercy of God, rest in peace.
R. Amen.

LITANY OF THE
SACRED HEART OF JESUS.

LORD have mercy.
Lord have mercy.
Christ have mercy.
Christ have mercy.
Lord have mercy.
Lord have mercy.
Christ hear us.
Christ, graciously hear us.
God the Father of heaven,
God the Son, Redeemer of the world,
God the Holy Ghost,
Holy Trinity, one God,
Heart of Jesus,
Heart of Jesus, hypostatically united with the word of God.
Heart of Jesus, Sanctuary of the Divinity,
Heart of Jesus, Temple of the Holy Trinity,
Heart of Jesus, Abyss of wisdom,

Have mercy on us.

LITANY OF THE

Heart of Jesus, Ocean of goodness,
Heart of Jesus, Throne of mercy,
Heart of Jesus, Treasure inexhaustible,
Heart of Jesus, of whose fullness we have all received,
Heart of Jesus, our Peace and our Atonement,
Heart of Jesus, Model of all virtues,
Heart of Jesus, infinitely loving, and infinitely worthy of love,
Heart of Jesus, Fountain of water springing up into everlasting life,
Heart of Jesus, in which the Father is well pleased,
Heart of Jesus, the Propitiation for our sins,
Heart o Jesus, filled with bitterness for our sakes,
Heart of Jesus, sorrowful in the Garden even unto death,
Heart of Jesus, saturated with revilings,
Heart of Jesus, wounded with love,
Heart of Jesus, pierced with a lance,
Heart of Jesus, exhausted of thy blood upon the Cross,
Heart of Jesus, bruised for our sins,
Heart of Jesus, still outraged by ungrateful men in the most holy Sacrament of love,
Heart of Jesus, Refuge of sinners,
Heart of Jesus, Strength of the weak,
Heart of Jesus, Comfort of the afflicted,
Heart of Jesus, Perseverance of the just,

Have mercy on us.

SACRED HEART OF JESUS.

Heart of Jesus, Salvation of them that hope in thee,
Heart of Jesus, Hope of them that die in thee,
Heart of Jesus, sweet support of those who worship thee,
Heart of Jesus, our Helper in our many and great tribulations,
Heart of Jesus, delight of all the Saints,

Have mercy on us.

Lamb of God, who takest away the sins of the world, *Spare us, O Lord.*
Lamb of God, who takest away the sins of the world,
Graciously hear us, O Lord.
Lamb of God, who takest away the sins of the world, *Have mercy on us.*
Christ, hear us,
Christ, graciously hear us.
V. Jesus, who art meek and humble of heart,
R. Make our hearts like unto thy Heart.

Let us Pray.

GRANT, we beseech thee, Almighty God, that, as, in worshipping the most sacred Heart of thy well-beloved Son, we call to mind the special benefits which his love hath bestowed upon us, so we may ever enjoy the fruits which flow therefrom. Through the same Christ our Lord. Amen.

LITANY OF THE
SACRED HEART OF MARY.

LORD have mercy.
Lord have mercy.
Christ have mercy.
Christ have mercy.
Lord have mercy.
Lord have mercy.
Christ hear us.
Christ, graciously hear us.
God the Father of heaven, *Have mercy on us.*
God the Son, Redeemer of the world, *Have mercy on us.*
God the Holy Ghost, *Have mercy on us.*
Holy Trinity, one God, *Have mercy on us.*
Heart of Mary,
Heart of Mary, according to the Heart of God,
Heart of Mary, united to the Heart of Jesus,
Heart of Mary, organ of the Holy Ghost,
Heart of Mary, sanctuary of the Divine Trinity,
Heart of Mary, tabernacle of God incarnate,
Heart of Mary, immaculate from thy creation,
Heart of Mary, full of grace,
Heart of Mary, blessed among all hearts,
Heart of Mary, throne of glory,
Heart of Mary, abyss of humility,

Pray for us.

SACRED HEART OF MARY. 281

Heart of Mary, holocaust of divine love,
Heart of Mary, fastened to the cross with Jesus crucified,
Heart of Mary, comfort of the afflicted,
Heart of Mary, refuge of sinners,
Heart of Mary, hope of the agonizing,
Heart of Mary, seat of mercy,

Pray for us.

Lamb of God, who takest away the sins of the world,
Spare us, O Lord.
Lamb of God, who takest away the sins of the world,
Graciously hear us, O Lord.
Lamb of God, who takest away the sins of the world,
Have mercy on us.
Christ, hear us.
Christ, graciously hear us.
V. Immaculate Mary, meek and humble of heart.
R. Make our heart according to the Heart of Jesus.

Let us Pray.

O most merciful God, who, for the salvation of sinners and the refuge of the miserable, wast pleased that the Immaculate Heart of the blessed Virgin Mary should be most like in charity and pity to the Divine Heart of thy Son Jesus-Christ; grant that we, who commemorate this most sweet and loving Heart, may, by the merits and intercession of the same blessed Virgin, merit to be found according to the Heart of Jesus. Through the same Christ our Lord. Amen.

LITANY OF THE
IMMACULATE CONCEPTION.

LORD have mercy.
Lord have mercy.
Christ have mercy.
Christ have mercy.
Lord have mercy.
Lord have mercy.
Christ hear us.
Christ, graciously hear us.
God the Father, Source of all sanctity,
God the Son, increated Sanctity,
God the Holy Ghost, Spirit of sanctity,
Most sacred Trinity, one God,
Holy Mary, immaculate,
Holy Virgin, by predestination immaculate,
Holy Virgin, in thy conception immaculate,
Holy Virgin, after thy conception immaculate,
Daughter of the Father, immaculate,
Mother of the Son, immaculate,
Spouse of the Holy Ghost, immaculate,
Seat of the most holy Trinity, immaculate,
Image of the Wisdom of God, immaculate,

Have, &c.

Pray for us.

IMMACULATE CONCEPTION. 283

Dawn of the Sun of Justice, immaculate,
Living Ark of the body of Christ, immaculate,
Daughter of David, immaculate,
Guide to Jesus, immaculate,
Virgin triumphing over original sin, immaculate,
Virgin, crushing the head of the serpent, immaculate,
Queen of heaven and earth, immaculate,
Gate of the heavenly Jerusalem, immaculate,
Dispenser of graces, immaculate,
Spouse of St. Joseph, immaculate,
Star of the world, immaculate,
Impregnable tower of the Church militant, immaculate,
Rose amid thorns, immaculate,
Olive of the fields, immaculate,
Model of all perfection, immaculate,
Cause of our hope, immaculate,
Pillar of our faith, immaculate,
Source of divine love, immaculate,
Sure sign of our salvation, immaculate,
Rule of perfect obedience, immaculate,
Pattern of holy poverty, immaculate,
School of devotion, immaculate,
Abode of chaste modesty, immaculate,
Anchor of our salvation, immaculate,
Light of Angels, immaculate,
Crown of Patriarchs, immaculate,
Glory of Prophets, immaculate,

Pray for us.

Lady and Mistress of Apostles, immaculate,
Support of Martyrs, immaculate,
Strength of Confessors, immaculate,
Diadem of Virgins, immaculate,
Splendor of all Saints, immaculate,
Sanctity of all Christians, immaculate,
Companion of devout souls, immaculate,
Joy of those who hope in thee, immaculate,
Health of the sick, immaculate,
Advocate of sinners, immaculate,
Terror of heretics, immaculate,
Protectress of all mankind, immaculate,
Patroness of those who honor thee, immaculate,

Pray for us.

Lamb of God, who takest away the sins of the world, *Spare us, O Lord.*

Lamb of God, who takest away the sins of the world,

Graciously hear us, O Lord.

Lamb of God, who takest away the sins of the world,

Have mercy on us.

V. In thy conception, O Virgin Mary, then wast immaculate.

R. Pray for us to the Father, whose son Jesus, conceived of the Holy Ghost, thou didst bring forth.

Pope Pius VI granted an indulgence of one hundred days, to be gained each time the above V. and R. are recited with devotion and contrition.

CHILDREN OF MARY. 285

Let us Pray.

O ALMIGHTY and Eternal God, who didst prepare for thy Son a worthy habitation, by the immaculate conception of the blessed Virgin Mary; we beseech thee, that, as thou didst preserve her from every stain of sin, through the merits of the pre-ordained atonement of Jesus Christ, so thou wouldst grant, that we also may come without spot to thee. Through the same Jesus Christ our Lord. Amen.

LITANY OF THE CHILDREN OF MARY.

LORD have mercy on us.
Christ have mercy on us.
Daughter of God the Father, elevated above all creatures, govern *Thy children.*
Mother of God the Son, and our Mother, protect *Thy children.*
Spouse of the Holy Ghost, obtain the sanctification of *Thy children.*
Mother of strength, obtain for thy children the gift of perseverance and courage,
Mother of love, obtain for thy children a true, generous, and constant love of God,
Mother, full of zeal for the glory of thy Divine Son, obtain for thy children the gift of a lively, prudent, and enlightened zeal,
Mother, who didst preserve thyself as pure as the lily in the midst of thorns, obtain

O Mary, hear us!

for thy children a love of Purity which may preserve them from all sin,

Mother, who didst never lose sight of the presence of God, obtain for thy children the grace ever to remember Him, even amidst the tumults of this world,

Mother most generous, obtain for thy children patience and resignation in all the trials of this life,

Mother, ever calm, even at the foot of the cross obtain for thy children the spirit of peace, which may sustain us amidst the afflictions of life,

Mother most faithful, obtain for thy children a lively faith that they may behold, God in all his creatures,

Mother most meek and humble, obtain for thy children the virtues of meekness and humility,

Mother, who in all thy actions sought to please thy God, obtain for thy children purity of intention and may our conduct prove as thy true children,

Mother, who didst despise the world and its vanities, obtain for thy children the grace to resist its deceitful charms,

By thy Immaculate Conception, O mother hear thy children!

By the fervor with which thou didst offer thyself to God at the age of three years, O mother hear thy children!

O thou who wert ever resigned to God's holy will, obtain for thy children perfect conformity to the will of God,
O Mother, hear us!
By thy heart pierced with a sword of grief,
O Mother, hear us!
O thou who never forsakest those who confide in thee, protect us from the snares of our enemy,
O Mother, hear us!
St. Joseph, faithfull guardian of Jesus and Mary, *Pray for us.*
Saints Aloysius and Stanislaus, devoted servants of Mary, *Pray for us.*
Lamb of God, who thakest away the sins of the world,
Hear us, O Lord.
Lamb of God, who takest away the sins of the world,
Spare us, O Lord.
Lam of God, who takest away the sins of the world,
Have mercy on us.
Jesus, hear us.
Jesus, graciously hear us.
O Mary, full of grace, look down upon and bless thy children.

Let us Pray.

O JESUS, who from the cross didst give Mary to be the Mother of mankind, and hast placed us

LITANY OF THE

among her privileged children, grand that, profiting by the graces thou hast so abundantly shed upon us, we may realize the consoling words : « It is impossible that a true servant of Mary should perish. » We ask it, O Jesus, by the tenderness of thy divine Heart, and the merits of thy Holy Passion.

LITANY OF THE

HOLY ANGEL GUARDIAN.

Lord have mercy.
Lord have mercy.
Christ have mercy.
Christ have mercy.
Lord have mercy.
Lord have mercy.
Christ hear us.
Christ graciously hear us.
God the Father of heaven, *Have mercy on us.*
God the Son, Redeemer of the world, *Have mercy on us.*
God the Holy Ghost, *Have mercy on us.*
Holy Trinity, one God, *Have mercy on us.*
Holy Mary, Queen of Angels,
Holy Angel, my guardian,
Holy Angel, my prince,
Holy Angel, my monitor,
Holy Angel, my counsellor,

Pray for us.

HOLY ANGEL GUARDIAN.

Holy Angel, my defender,
Holy Angel, my steward,
Holy Angel, my friend,
Holy Angel, my negotiator,
Holy Angel, my intercessor,
Holy Angel, my patron,
Holy Angel, my director,
Holy Angel, my ruler,
Holy Angel, my protector,
Holy Angel, my comforter,
Holy Angel, my brother,
Holy Angel, my teacher,
Holy Angel, my shepherd,
Holy Angel, my witness,
Holy Angel, my helper,
Holy Angel, my watcher.
Holy Angel, my conductor,
Holy Angel, my preserver,
Holy Angel, my instructor,
Holy Angel, my enlightener,

Pray for us.

Lamb of God, who takest away the sins of the world,
Spare us, O Lord.
Lamb of God, who takest away the sins of the world,
Graciously hear us, O Lord.
Lamb of God, who takest away the sins of the world,
Have mercy on us.
Christ hear us,

Christ graciously hear us.
V. Pray for us, O holy Angel-guardian,
R. That we may be made worthy of the promises of Christ.

Let us pray.

ALMIGHTY, everlasting God, who, in the counsel of thy ineffable goodness, hast appointed to all the faithful, from their mother's womb, a special Angel-guardian of their body and soul; grant that I may so love and honor him whom thou hast so mercifully given me, that, protected by the bounty of thy grace, and by his assistance, I may merit to behold, with him and all the angelic host, the glory of thy countenance in the heavenly country. Who livest and reignest, world without end. Amen.

LITANY OF ST. JOSEPH.

LORD have mercy.
Lord have mercy.
Christ have mercy.
Christ have mercy.
Lord have mercy.
Lord have mercy.
Christ hear us.
Christ graciously hear us.
God the Father of heaven, *Have mercy on us.*

LITANY OF ST. JOSEPH. 291

God the Son, Redeemer of the world, *Have mercy on us.*
God the Holy Ghost, *Have mercy on us.*
Holy Trinity, one God, *Have mercy on us.*
Holy Mary, Spouse of Joseph,
Holy Joseph, Spouse of the Virgin Mary,
Nursing-father of Jesus,
Man according to God's own heart,
Faithful and prudent servant,
Guardian of the virginity of Mary,
Companion and solace of Mary,
Most pure in virginity,
Most profound in humility,
Most fervent in charity,
Most exalted in contemplation,
Who whast declared to be a just man by the testimony of the Holy Ghost himself,
Who wast enlightened above all the heavenly mysteries,
Who wast the chosen minister of the counsels of the Most High,
Who wast taught from above the mystery of the Incarnate Word,
Who didst journey to Bethlehem with Mary thy Spouse, being great with child,
Who finding no place in the inn, didst betake thyself to a stable,
Who wast thought worthy to be present when Christ was born and laid in a manger,
Who didst bear in thine arms the Son of God,

Pray for us.

LITANY OF ST. JOSEPH.

Who didst receive the blood of Jesus at his Circumcision,
Who didst present him to the Lord in the Temple, with Mary his Mother,
Who, at the warning of the Angel, didst fly into Egypt with the Child and his Mother,
Who, when Herod was dead, didst return with them into the land of Israel,
Who for three days, with Mary his Mother didst seek sorrowing the Child Jesus, when he was last at Jerusalem,
Who, after three days, didst find him with joy sitting in the midst of the Doctors,
Who hadst the Lord of lords subject to thee on the earth,
Who wast the happy witness of his hidden life and sacred words,
Who didst die in the arms of Jesus and Mary,
Whose praise is in the Gospel: The Husband of Mary, of whom was born Jesus,.
Humble imitator of the Incarnate Word,
Powerful support of the Church,
Our advocate, *St. Joseph, hear us.*
Our patron, *St. Joseph, graciously hear us.*
In all our necessities,
In all our distresses,
In the our of death,
Through thy most chaste espousals,
Through thy paternal care and fidelity,
Through thy love of Jesus and Mary,

LITANY OF ST. JOSEHP.

Through thy labors and toils, *St. Joseph, hear us.*
Through all thy virtues, *St Joseph, hear us.*
Through thy exalted honor and eternal blessedness, *St. Joseph, hear us.*
Through thy faithful intercession, *St. Joseph, hear us.*
We, thy clients, *Beseech thee, hear us.*
That thou wouldst vouchsafe to obtain for us, from Jesus, the pardon of our sins,
That thou wouldst vouchsafe to commend us faithfully to Jesus and Mary,
That thou wouldst vouchsafe to obtain for all, both Virgins and married, the chastity belonging to their state,
That thou wouldst vouchsafe to obtain for all congregations perfect love and concord,
That thou wouldst vouchsafe to direct all rulers and prelates in the government of their subjects,
That thou wouldst vouchsafe to assist all parents in the Christian education of their children,
That thou wouldst vouchsafe to protect all those that rely upon thy patronage,
That thou wouldst vouchsafe to support, with thy paternal help, all congregations instituted under thy name and patronage,
That thou wouldst vouchsafe to visit and stand by us, with Jesus and Mary, in the last moment of our life,

We beseech thee, hear us.

That thou wouldst vouchsafe to succor, by thy prayers and intercession, all the faithful departed, *We beseech thee hear us.*
O chaste Spouse of Mary. *We beseech thee,* &c.
O faithful Nursing-father of Jesus, *We beseech thee, hear us.*
Holy Joseph, *We beseech thee, hear us.*

Lamb of God who takest away the sins of the world, *Spare us, O Lord.*

Lamb of God, who takest away the sins of the world, *Graciously hear us, O Lord.*

Lamb of God, who takest away the sins of the world, *Have mercy on us.*

Christ hear us,
Christ graciously hear us.
V. Pray for us, O blessed Joseph.
R. That we may be made worthy of the promises of Christ.

Let us Pray.

O GOD, who didst choose St. Joseph to be the Spouse of blessed Mary ever Virgin, and to be the Guardian and Nursing father of thy beloved Son, our Lord Jesus Christ; we humbly beseech thee to grant us, through his patronage and merits, such purity of mind and body, that, being clean from every stain, and clothed with the true marriage-garment, we may, by thy great mercy, be admitted to the heavenly nuptials. Through the same Christ our Lord. Am.

Litany of St. Vincent of Paul.

LORD have mercy.
Lord have mercy.
Christ have mercy.
Christ have mercy.
Lord have mercy.
Lord have mercy.
Christ hear us.
Christ graciously hear us.
God the Father of heaven, *Have mercy on us.*
God the Son, Redeemer of the world, *Have mercy on us.*
God the Holy Ghost, *Have mercy on us.*
Holy Trinity, one God, *Have mercy on us.*
Holy Mary,
St. Vincent of Paul,
St. Vincent, who at the tenderest age didst display a wisdom most mature,
St. Vincent, who, from thy childhood, wast full of piety and compassion,
St. Vincent, who, like David, from a simple shepherd becamest the ruler and pastor of the people of God,
St. Vincent, who in thy captivity didst preserve a perfect freedom,
St. Vincent, the just man, who livedst by faith,

Pray for us.

*This Litany is intended especially for the members of the Brotherhood of St. Vincent of Paul.

LITANY OF

St. Vincent, always supported on the firm anchor of a Christian hope,
St. Vincent, always inflamed with the fire of charity,
St. Vincent, truly simple, upright, and fearing God.
St Vincent, true disciple of Jesus-Christ, always meek and humble of heart.
St. Vincent, perfectly mortified in heart and mind,
St. Vincent, ever animated with the spirit of Jesus-Christ,
St. Vincent, generous maintainer of the glory of God,
St. Vincent, ever inwardly burning and ever outwardly transported, with zeal for souls,
St. Vincent, who in Christian poverty didst find the precious pearl, and the rich treasure of the Gospel,
St. Vincent, like to the Angels in thy purity,
St. Vincent, ever faithful in obedience, and ever victorious in word,
St. Vincent, from thy earliest years constantly devoted to works of charity.
St. Vincent, who didst fly with most dilligent care the slightest appearance of evil,
St. Vincent, who, in all thine actions, didst aspire to the practice of the most perfect virtue,
St. Vincent, who, like a rock, remainedst immovable amidst the stormy sea of this world.

Pray for us.

St Vincent, who, constant as the sun in its course, wentest ever onward in the paths of truest wisdom,

St. Vincent, always invincible by all the arrows of adversity,

St Vincent, as patient in suffering as thou wast indulgent in forgiving,

St. Vincent, ever docile and obedient son of the Holy Romain Church.

St. Vincent, who hadst exceeding horror of the novel ways and subtle words of heresy,

St. Vincent, destined by a special Providence to announce the Gospel to the poor,

St. Vincent, tender father and perfect model of ecclesiastics,

St. Vincent, prudent founder of the Congregation of the Mission,

St. Vincent, wise institutor of the order Sisters of Charity,

St. Vincent, always tender in compassionating, and always prompt in relieving, all the necessities of the poor,

St. Vincent, equally fervent in the practise of prayer and in the ministry of the word,

St. Vincent, perfect imitator of the life and virtues of Jesus Christ,

St. Vincent, who didst persevere to the end in eschewing evil and doing good,

St. Vincent, who, as in life so in death, wast most precious in the sight of God,

Pray for us

(St. Vincent, who by the knowledge of absolute truth, by the love of sovereign goodness, by the joys of a blessed eternity, posessest perfect happiness,
Pray for the members of the Church, and expecially for the membres of this brotherhood.)
Lamb of God who takest away the sins of the world, *Spare us, o Lord.*
Lamb of God who takest away the sins of the world,
Graciously hear us, O Lord.
Lamb of God who takest away the sins of the world,
Have mercy on us.
V. The Lord had led the just man through right ways.
R. And showed unto him the kingdom of God.

Let us Pray.

GREAT God, who, by an effect of hine infinite goodness, has renewed, in our days, in the apostolic charity and humilty of thy blessed servant Vincent, the spirit of thy well-beloved Son to preach the Gospel to the poor, relieve the afflicted, console the miserable, and add new lustre to the ecclesiastical order; grant, we beseech thee, through his powerful intercession, that we also, being delivered from the great misery of sin, may labor to please thee by the practise of the same humility. Through Jesus Christ our Lord, &c. Amen.

LITANY OF ST. ALOYSIUS.

LORD have mercy on us.
Lord have mercy on us.
Christ have mercy on us.
Christ have mercy on us.
Lord have mercy on us.
Lord have mercy on us.
Christ hear us.
Christ graciously hear us.
God the Father of heaven, *Have mercy on us.*
God the Son, Redeemer of the world, *Have mercy on us.*
God the Holy Ghost, *Have mercy on us.*
Holy Trinity, one God, *Have mercy on us.*
Holy Mary,
Holy Mother of God,
Holy Virgin of Virgins,
St. Aloysius,
Most beloved of Christ,
The delight of the Blessed Virgin,
Most chaste youth,
Angelic youth,
Most humble youth,
Model of young students,
Despiser of riches,
Enemy of vanities,
Scorner of honors,
Honor of princes,

Pray for us.

LITANY OF ST. ALOYSIUS.

Jewel of the nobility,
Flower of innocence,
Ornement of a religious state,
Mirror of mortification,
Mirror of perfect obedience,
Lover of evangelical poverty,
Most affectionately devout,
Most zealous observer of rules,
Most desirous of the salvation of souls,
Perpetual adorer of the holy Eucharist,
Particular client of St. Ignatius,

Pray for us.

Be merciful spare us, O Lord.
Be merciful, hear us, O Lord.
From the concupiscence of the eyes,
From the concupiscence of the flesh,
From the pride of life,
Through the merits and intercession of Aloysius,
Through his angelical purity,
Through his sanctity and glory,

O Lord, &c.

We sinners, *Beseech thee hear us.*

Lamb of God, who takest away the sins of the world,
Spare us, O Lord.

Lamb of God, who takest away the sins of the world,
Hear us, O Lord.

Lamb of God, who takest away the sins of the world,
Have mercy on us.

Christ, hear us.
Christ, graciously hear us.
V. Pray for us, St. Aloysius.
R. That we may be made worthy of the promises of Christ.

Let us Pray.

O GOD! the distributor of heavenly gifts, who didst unite in the angelic youth Aloysius, wonderful innocence of life with an equal severity of penance, grant through his merits and prayers that we, who have not followed the example of his innocence, may imitate his practise of penance; through our Lord Jesus Christ. Amen.

LITANY FOR CHILDREN.

LORD have mercy on us.
Lord have mercy on us.
Christ have mercy on us.
Christ have mercy on us.
Lord have mercy on us.
Lord have mercy on us.
Jesus, almighty God,
Jesus, God of peace,
Jesus, lover of mankind,
Jesus, model of meekness and himility,
Jesus, model of innocence and simplicity,
Jesus, model of truth and sincerity,
Jesus, model of chastity and purity of heart,

Have mercy on us.

LITANY FOR CHILDREN.

Jesus, pattern of submission and obedience,
Jesus, pattern of mildness and gentleness,
Jesus, pattern of charity and goodwill to men,
Jesus, pattern of all virtues,
Be merciful, O Jesus, and spare us.
Be merciful, O Jesus, and hear us.
From all irreligion,
Lord Jesus, deliver us.
From profane ridicule and contempt of what is holy,
Lord Jesus, deliver us.
From the neglect of what we know to be our duty,
From carelessness in our devotions,
From the neglect of thy cals and inspirations,
From lying, deceit, and hypocrisy,
From disobedience to our parents and superiors,
From stubbornness and obstinacy,
From ingratitude to those who do us good,
From all hatred and ill-will,
From seeking revenge,
From a heedless and unthinking life,
From too great a love of ourselves and our own wils,
From inattention to learning and the instructions of our superiors,
From all loss of the valuable time of youth,
We sinners, *beseech thee, hear us.*
That we may love thee above all things, and

LITANY FOR CHILDREN.

our neighbor as ourselves, *We beseech thee hear us.*

That our love of thee may show itself in the observance of thy commandments,

That the love of our neighbor may appear in always doing to him as we wish him to do to us,

That we may be grateful to thee, the giver of all good gifts,

That we may live soberly, justly, and godly; and keep our thougths free from all the defilement of sin,

That our thougtbs, words, and actions, may be directed to thee, who art the author of life here, and happiness hereafter.

That we may make a good use of our advantages, by seeking instruction, loving our prayers, our learning, and all other duties,

That we may hate idleness, as the source of much wickedness,

That the spirit of mildness and gentleness may appear in all our actions,

That we may bear with others' failings, as we wish them to bear with our own,

That we may live together as brothers, children of the same Father, and looking for the blessed hope, and coming of thee, our Lord and Saviour Jesus Christ,

Lamb of God, who takest away the sins of the world,

LITANY FOR CHILDREN.

Spare us, O Lord Jesus.
Lamb of God, who takest away the sins of the world,
Hear us, O Lord Jesus.
Lamb of God, who takest away the sins of the world,
Have mercy on us, O Lord Jesus.
Christ Jesus, hear us.
Christ Jesus, graciously hear us.

Let us Pray.

O JESUS, our merciful Redeemer, who didst call children to thee, didst embrace them, and give them thy blessing, give thy blessing to us also, we beseech thee, this day, and through the course of our lives. Grant that we may ever love thee above all things, and with our whole hearts; that we may love our neighbor as ourselves, and ardently aspire after that happines for which we were created.

Bless our parents, teachers relations, and benefactors : preserve them from evil, and direct them to all good; and grant that we may all meet together in thy eternal kingdom. Amen.

The Seven Penitential Psalms.

PROPER TO BE RECITED ON
Fasting Days, and at other Penitential Times.

ANTHEM.

REMEMBER not, O Lord, our offences, nor those of our parents, and take not revenge on our sins.

PSALM 6. — *Domine, ne in furore.*

1. David, in deep affliction, prays for a mitigation of the divine anger; 4. in consideration of God's mercy; 5. His glory; 6. his own repentance; 8. by faith triumphs over his enemies.

O LORD, rebuke me not in thy indignation, nor chastise me in Thy wrath.

Have mercy on me, O Lord, for I am weak: heal me, O Lord, for my bones are troubled.

And my soul is troubled exceedingly: but Thou, O Lord, how long?

Turn to me, O Lord, and deliver my soul: O save me for Thy mercy's sake.

For there is no one in death that is mindful of Thee and who shall confess to Thee in hell?

I have labored in my groanings, every

night I will wash my bed, I will water my couch with my tears.

My eye is troubled through indignation : I have grown old among all may enemies.

Depart from me, all ye workers of iniquity: for the Lord hath heard the voice of my weeping.

The Lord hath heard my supplication : the Lord hath received my prayer.

Let my enemies be ashamed, and be very much troubled : let them be turned back, and be ashamed very speedily.

Glory be, & c.

PSALM 31. — *Beati quorum.*

4. Blessings of remission of sins ; 3. misery of impenitence ; 6. confession of sins bringeth ease, 8. safety ; 14. joy.

Blessed are thy whose iniquities are forgiven, and whose sins are covered.

Blessed is the man to whom the Lord hath not imputed sin, and in whose spirit there is no guile.

Because I was silent, my bones grew old ; whilst I cried out all the day long.

For day and night Thy hand was heavy

upon me : I am turned in my anguish, whilst the thorn is fastened.

I have acknowledged my sin to Thee ; and my injustice I have not concealed.

I said I will confess against myself my injustice to the Lord, and Thou hast forgiven the wickedness of my sin.

For this shall every one that is holy pray to Thee, in a seasonable time.

And yet in a flood of many waters, they shall not come nigh unto Him.

Thou art my refuge from the trouble which hath encompassed me ; my joy, deliver me from them that surround me.

I will give thee understanding, and I will instruct thee in the way in which thou shalt go ; I will fix my eyes upon thee.

Do not become like the horse and the mule that have no understanding.

With bit and bridle bind fast their jaws who come not near unto thee.

Many are the scourges of the sinner, but mercy shall encompass him that hopeth in the Lord.

Be glad in the Lord, and rejoice ye just, and glory, all ye right of heart.

Glory be, &c.

PSALM 37. — *Domine, ne in furore.*

1. David's extreme anguish ; 15. he hopeth in God ; 18. his resignation, grief ; 22. fervent prayer.

Rebuke me not, O Lord, in Thy indignation, nor chastise me in Thy wrath.

For Thy arrows are fastened in me; and Thy hand hath been strong upon me.

There is no health in my flesh, because of Thy wrath ; there is no peace for my bones, because of my sins.

For my iniquities are gone over my head; and as a heavy burden are become heavy upon me.

My sores are putrified and corrupted, because of my foolishness.

I am become miserable, and am bowed down even to the end ; I walked sorrowful all the day long.

For my loins are filled with illusions ; and there is no health in my flesch.

I am afficted and humbled exceedingly ; I roared with the groaning of my heart.

Lord, all my desire is before Thee ; and my groaning is not hid from thee.

My heart is troubled, my strength hath left me, and the light of my eyes itself is not with me.

My friends and my neighbors have drawn near, and stood against me.

And they that were near me stood afar off; and they that sought my soul used violence.

And they that sought evils to me spoke vain things, and studied deceits all the day long.

But I, as a deaf man, heard not; and as a dumb man not opening his mouth.

And I became as a man that heareth not; and that hath no reproofs in his mouth.

For in thee, O Lord, have I hoped; Thou wilt hear me, O Lord, my God.

For I said, Lest at any time my enemies rejoice over me; and whilst my feet are moved, they speak great things against me.

For I am ready for scourges; and my sorrow is continually before me.

For I will declare my iniquity; and I will think for my sin.

But my enemies live, and are stronger than I; and they that hate me wrongfully are multiplied.

They that render evil for good, have detracted me, because I followed goodness.

Forsake me not, O Lord my God; do no Thou depart from me.

Attend unto my help, O Lord, the God of my salvation.

Glory be, etc.

PSALM 50. — *Miserere.*

1. David prayeth for remission of his sins; 8. for perfect sanctity; 17. God delighteth not in sacrifice, but a contrite heart; 19. he prayeth for the building of a temple in Jerusalem, figuratively, the exaltation of the Church.

Have mercy on me, O God, according to thy great mercy.

And according to the multitude of Thy tender mercies, blot out my iniquity.

Wash me yet more from my iniquity, and cleanse me from my sin.

For I know my iniquity, and my sin is always before me.

To Thee only have I sinned, and have done evil before Thee; that Thou mayest be justified in Thy words, and mayest overcome when Thou art judged.

For behold I was conceived in iniquities; and in sins did my mother conceive me.

For behold Thou hast loved truth; the uncertain and hidden things of Thy wisdom Thou hast made manifest to me.

Thou shalt sprinkle me with hyssop, and I

shall be cleansed. Thou shalt wash me, and I shall be made whiter than snow.

To my hearing Thou shalt give joy and gladness : and the bones that have been humbled shall rejoice.

Turn away Thy face from my sins, and blot out all my iniquities.

Create a clean heart in me, O God, and renew a right spirit within my bowels.

Cast me not away from Thy face; and take not Thy Holy spirit from me.

Restore unto me the joy of Thy salvatisn, and strengthen me with a perfect spirit.

I will teach the unjust Thy ways; and the wicked shall be converted to Thee.

Deliver me from blood, O God, Thou God of my salvation; and my tongue shall extol Thy justice.

O Lord, Thou wilt open my lips; and my mouth shall declare Thy praise.

For if Thou hadst desired sacrifice, I would indeed have given it; with burnt-offerings Thou wilt not be delighted.

A sacrifice to God is an afflicted spirit; a contrite and humble heart, o God, Thou wilt not dispise.

Deal favorably, O Lord, in thy good-will with

Sion; that the walls of Jerusalem may be built up.

Then shalt Thou accept the sacrifice of justice, oblations, and whole burnt-offerings, then shall they lay calves upon Thy altar.

Glory be, &c.

PSALM 101 — *Domine, exaudi.*

1. The extreme affliction of the Psalmist; 12. the eternity and mercy of God; 19. to be recorded, and praised by future generations; 26. the unchangeableness of God.

Hear, O Lord, my prayer, and let my cry come to Thee.

Turn not away Thy face from me; in the day when I am troubled, incline Thine ear to me.

In what day soever I shall call upon Thee, hear me speedily.

For my das are vanished like smoke; and my bones are grown dry like fuel for the fire.

I am smitten as grass, and my heart is withered; because I forgot to eat my bread.

Through the voice of my groaning my bone hath cleaved to my flesh.

I am become like to a pelican of the wilderness; I am like a night-raven in the house.

I have watched, and am become as a sparrow, all alone on the house-top.

All the day long my enemies reproach me; and they that praised me did swear against me.

For I did eat ashes like bread; and mingled my drink with weeping.

Because of Thy anger and indignation; for having lifted me up Thou hast trown me down.

My days have declined like a shadow; and I am withered like grass.

But Thou, O Lord, endurest for ever; and Thy memorial to all generations.

Thou shalt arise and have mercy on Sion, for it is time to have mercy on it, for the time is come.

For the stones thereof have pleased Thy servants, and they shall have pity on the earth thereof.

And the Gentiles shall fear Thy name, O Lord, and all the kings of the earth Thy glory.

For the Lord hath built up Sion; and He shall be seen in His glory.

He hath had regard to the prayer of the humble, and He hath not despised their petition.

Let these things be written unto anothe generation: and the people, that shall be cre ted, shall praise the Lord.

Because He hath looked forth from His high sanctuary; from heaven the Lord hath looked upon the earth.

That He might hear the groans of them that are in fetters; that He might release the chilldren of the slain.

That they may declare the name of the Lord in Sion, and His praise in Jerusalem.

When the people assembled together, and kings to serve the Lord.

He answered Him in the way of his strength : Declare unto me the fewness of my days.

Call me not away in the midst of my days : Thy years are unto generation and generation.

In the beginning, O Lord, Thou foundest the earth ; and the heavens are the works of Thy hands.

They shall perish, but Thou remainest : and all of them shall grow old like a garment.

And as a vesture Thou shalt change them, and they shall be changed; but Thou art always the self-same, and Thy years shall not fail.

The children of Thy servants shall continue : and their seed shall be directed for ever.

Glory be, &c.

PENITENTIAL PSALMS. 315

PSALM 129.— *De profundis.*

An excellent model for sinners imploring the divine mercy.

Out of the depths I have cried to thee, O Lord; Lord, hear my voice.

Let Thy ears be attentive to the voice of my supplication.

If Thou, O Lord, wilt mark iniquities, Lord, who shall stand it!

For with Thee there is merciful forgiveness: and by reason of Thy law I have waited for Thee, O Lord.

My soul hath relied on His word; my soul hath hoped in the Lord.

From the morning watch even until night, let Israel hope in the Lord.

Because with the Lord there is mercy, and with Him plentiful redemption.

And He shall redeem Israel from all his iniquities.

Glory be, &c.

PSALM 142 —*Domine, exaudi.*

1. David prayeth for favor in judgment; 3. represents his distress; 7. He prayeth for grace; 9. for deliverance; 10, for sanctification; 12. victory over his enemies.

Hear, O Lord, my prayer; give ear to my

supplication in Thy truth; hear me in Thy justice.

And enter not into judgment with Thy servant; for in Thy sight no man living shall be justified.

For the enemy hath persecuted my soul : he hath brought down my life to the earth.

He hath made me to dwell in darkness, as those that have been dead of old; and my spirit is in anguish within me! my heart within me is troubled.

I remembered the days of old, I mediated on all Thy works : I mused upon the works of Thy hands.

I stretched forth my hands to Thee : my soul is as earth without water unto thee.

Hear me speedily, O Lord; my spirit hath fainted away.

Turn not away Thy face from me, lest I be like unto them that go down into the pit.

Cause me to hear Thy mercy in the morning; for in Thee have I hoped.

Make the way known to me wherein I should walk; for I have lifted up my soul to Thee.

Deliver me from my enemies, O Lord, to Thee

PENITENTIAL PSALMS. 317

have I fled ; teach me to do Thy will, for Thou art my God.

Thy good spirit shall lead me into the right land ; for thy name's sake, O Lord, Thou wilt quicken me in Thy justice.

Thou wilt bring my soul out of troubles : and in Thy mercy Thou wilt destroy my enemies.

And Thou wilt cut off all them that afflict my soul : for I am Thy servant.

Glory be to the Father, & c.

ANTHEM.

REMEMBER not, O Lord, our offences, nor those of our parents ; and take not revenge on our sins.

VESPERS
FOR SUNDAYS AND FESTIVALS.

NEXT to the Sacrifice of the Mass, the Vespers, or evening office of the Church, is the most solemn act of public devotion you can perform. Assist at them, therefore, with all reverence and attention; and while the choir is singing the psalms and hymns of the day, unite yourself in spirit with the choir of Angels and Saints who are for ever singing the praises of God in heaven.

Pater noster, Ave Maria, in secret.

V. Deus, in adjutorium meum intende.

R. Domine, ad adjuvandum me festina.

V. Gloria Patri, et Filio, et Spiritui Sancto.

R. Sicut erat in

V. O God, come to my assistance.

R. O Lord, make haste to help me.

V. Glory be to the Father, and to the Son, and to the Holy Ghost.

R. As it was in

principio, et nunc, et semper, et in sæcula sæculorum. — Amen. Alleluia.

the beginning, is now, and ever shall be, world without end. Amen. Alleluia.

From Septuagesima to Palm Sunday, inclusively, is said :

Laus tibi, Domine, Rex æternæ gloriæ.
Ant. Dixit Dominus.

Praise be to thee. O Lord, King of everlasting glory.
Ant. The Lord said.

In Paschal Time, the Psalms are all said under this one Antiphon : *Alleluia.*

PSALM 109. *Dixit Dominus.*

Dixit Dóminus Dómino meo : * Sede a dextris meis :
Donec ponam inimicos tuos : * scabéllum pedum tuórum.

1. The Lord said to my Lord : Sit thou at my right hand :
2. Until I make thine enemies : thy footstool.

Virgam virtútis tuæ emíttet Dóminus ex Sion : * domináre in médio inimicòrum tuórum.

Tecum princípium in die virtútis tuæ, in splendóribus Sanctórum : * ex útero ante luciferum génui te.

Jurávit Dóminus, et non pœnitébit eum : * Tu es sacerdos in ætérnum, secúndum órdinem Melchísedech.

Dóminus a dextris tuis : * confrégit in die iræ suæ reges.

Judicábit in naẃónibus, implébit

3. The Lord shall send forth the rod of thy power from out of Sion : rule thou in the midst of thine enemies.

4. Thine shall be the dominion in the day of thy power, amid the brightness of the Saints : from the womb before the day-star have I begotten thee.

5. The Lord hath sworn, and will not repent: Thou art a priest for ever according to the order of Melchisedec.

6. The Lord upon thy right hand: hath overthrown kings in the day of his wrath.

7. He shall judge among the nations,

ruínas : * conquassábit cápita in terra multórum.

De torrénte in via bibit : * proptérea exaltábit caput.

Glória Patri, etc.

Ant. Dixit Dóminus Dómino meo: Sede a dextris meis.

Ant. Fidélia.

he shall fulfil destructions : he shall smite in sunder the heads in the land of many.
8. He shall drink of the brook in the way: therefore shall he lift up his head.

Glory be to the Father, &c.

Ant. The Lord said to my Lord : Sit thou at my right hand.

Ant. Faithful.

PSALM 110. — *Confitebor tibi.*

Confitébor tibi, Dómine, in toto corde meo : * in consílio justórum, et congregátione.

Magna ópera Do-

1. I will praise thee, O Lord, with my whole heart : in the assembly of the just, and in the congregátion.
2. Great are the

mini : * exquisíta in omnes voluntátes ejus.

Conféssio et magnificentia opus ejus: * et justítia ejus manet in sæculum sæculi.

Memóriam fecit mirabilium suórum miséricors et miserátor Dóminus : * escam dedit timéntibus se.

Memor erit in sæculum testaménti sui : * virtútem óperum suórum annuntiabit pópulo suo:

Ut det illis hæreditatem géntium : * opera manuum ejus véritas et judicium.

works of the Lord sought out are they unto all his pleasure.

3. His work is his praise and his honor : and his justice endureth for ever and ever.

4. The merciful and gracious Lord hath left a memorial of his marvelous works : he hath given meat to them that fear him.

5. He shall ever be mindful of his covenant : he shall show forth unto his people the power of his works :

6. That he may give them the heritage of the gentiles: the works of his hands are judgment and truth.

Fidélia ómnia mandáta ejus ; confirmáta in sæculum sæculi : * facta in veritáte et æquitate.

Redemptiónem misit pópulo suo : * mandavit in ætérnum testaméntum suum.

Sanctum et terribile nomen ejus : * initium sapiéntiæ timor Domini.

Intelléctus bonus ómnibus faciéntibus eum : * laudatio ejus manet in sæculum sæculi.

Glória Patri, &c.

Ant. Fidélia ómnia mandáta ejus,

7. Faithful are all his commandments; they stand fast for ever and ever : they are done in truth and equity.

8. He hath sent redemption unto his people : he hath commanded his covenant for ever.

9. Holy and terrible is his name : the fear of the Lord is the beginning of wisdom.

10. A good understanding have all they that do thereafter : his praise endureth for ever and ever.

Glory be to the Father, &c.

Ant. Faithful are all his command-

confirmáta in sæculum sæculi.

Ant. In mandatis.

ments; they stand fast for ever and ever.

Ant. In his commandments.

PSALM 111. — *Beatus vir.*

Béatus vir qui timet Dóminum : * in mandatis ejus volet nimis.

Potens in terra erit semen ejus : * generatio rectórum benedicetur.

Glória et divitiæ in domo ejus : * et justítia ejus manet in sæculum sæculi.

Exórtum est in ténebris lumen rectis : * miséricors, et

1. Blessed is the man that feareth the Lord ; in his commandments he shall have great delight.

2. His seed shall be mighty upon earth : the generation of the righteous shall be blessed.

3. Glory and riches shall be in his house : and his justice endureth for ever and ever.

5. Unto the righteous there hath risen up light in the

SUNDAYS AND FESTIVALS. 325

miserator, et justus.

Jucundus homo qui miserétur et cómmodat, dispónet sermónes suos in judício : * quia in ætérnum non comovébitur.

In memória ætérna erit justus : * ab auditióne mala non timébit.

Parátum cor ejus speráre in Dómino, confirmátum est cor ejus : * non commovébitur donec despíciat inimícos suos.

Dispérsit, dedit pauperibus ; justitio ejus manet in sæculum sæculi : *

darkness : he is merciful compassionate and just.

5. Acceptable is the man who is merciful, and lendeth ; he will guide his words with judgment : he shall not be moved for ever.

6. The just man shall be in everlasting remembrance : he shall not be afraid for evil report.

7. His heart is prepared to hope in the Lord ; his heart is fixed : he shall not be moved until he look down upon his enemies.

8. He hath dispersed abroad, he hath given to the poor ; his justice

Y

cornu ejus exaltábitur in glória.

Peccátor, vidébit et irascétur; déntibus suis fremet et tabéscet : * desidérium peccatórum períbit.

Glória Patri, & c.

Ant. In mandátis ejus capit nimis.
Ant. Sit nomen Dómini benedíctum.

endureth for ever and ever : his horn shall be exalted in glory.
9. The sinner shall see it, and be wroth : he shall gnash with his teeth, and consume away : the desire of the wicked shall perish.
Glory be to the Father, & c.
Ant. In his commandments he hath great delight.
Ant. Blessed be the name of the Lord.

Psalm 112. — *Laudate, pueri.*

Laudáte púeri, Dóminum : * laudate nomen Dómini.

1. Praise the Lord, ye children : praise ye the name of the Lord.

Sit nomen Dómini benedíctum : * ex hoc nunc et usque in sæculum.

A solis ortu usque ad accásum : * laudábile nomen Dómini.

Excelsus super omnes gentes Dóminus : * et super cœlos gloria ejus.

Quis sicut Dóminus Deus noster, qui in altis hábitat : * et humília réspicit in cœlo et in terra?

Súscitans a terra ínopem ; * et de stércore érigens

2. Blessed be the name of the Lord : from this time forth for evermore.

3. From the rising up of the sun unto the going down of the same : the name of the Lord is worthy to be praised.

4. The Lord is high above all nations : and his glory above the heavens.

5. Who is like unto the Lord our God who dwelleth on high : and regardeth the things that are lowly in heaven and in earth?

6. Who raiseth up the needy from the earth : and lift-

páuperem : | eth the poor from off the dunghill.

Ut cóllocet eum cum princípibus : * cum princípibus pópuli sui. | 7. That he may set him with the princes : even with the princes of his people.

Qui habtitáre facit stérilem in domo : * matrem filiórum lætantem. | 8. Who maketh the barren woman to dwell in her house ; the joyful mother of children.

Gloria Patri, &c. | Glory be to the Father, etc.

Ant. Sit nomen Dómini bénedíctum. | *Ant.* Blessed be the name of the Lord for ever.

Ant. Nos qui vívimus. | *Ant.* We who live.

PSALM 113. — *In exitu Israel.*

In éxitu Israel de Ægypto : * domus Jacob de pópulo barbaro. | 1. When Israel came out of Egypt; the house of Jacob from among a strange people.

SUNDAYS AND FESTIVALS. 329

Facta est Judæa sanctificátio ejus : * Israel potéstas ejus.

Mare vidit et fugit : * Jordánis convérsus est retrórsum

Montes exultavérunt ut aríetes : * et colles sicut agni óvium.

Quid est tibi, mare, quod fugusti : * et tu, Jordanis, quia convérsus es retrórsum ?

Montes, exultástis sicut aríetes : * et colles, sicut agni óvium ?

A fácie Dómini mota est terra : * a fácie Dei Jacob.

2. Judah was made his sanctuary : and Israel his dominion.

3. The sea beheld, and fled : Jordan was turned back.

4 The mountains skipped like rams : and te little hills like the lambs of the flock.

5. What aileth thee, O thou sea, that thou fleddest : and thou Jordan, that thou wast turned back ?

6. Ye mountains, that ye skipped like rams : and ye little hills like the lambs of the flock ?

7. At the presence of the Lord the earth was moved :

Qui convértit petram in stagna aquarum : * et rupem in fontes aquárum.

Non nobis Dómine, non nobis : * sed nómini tuo da glóriam.

Super misericórdia tua, et veritáte tua : * nequándo dicant gentes, Ubi est Deus eórum ?

Deus autem noster in cœlo : * ómnia quæcumque vóluit fecit.

Simulácra géntium argéntum et aurum : * ópera mánuum hóminum.

Os habent, et non

at the presence of the God of Jacob.

8. Who turned the rock into a standing water: and the stony hill into a flowing stream.

9. Not unto us, O Lord, not unto us : but unto thy name give the glory.

10. For thy mercy and for thy truth's sake: lest the gentiles should say, Where is their God?

11. But our God is in heaven : he hath done whatsoever he would.

12. The idols of the gentiles are silver and gold : the work of the hands of men.

13. They have

loquéntur : * óculos habent, et non vidébunt.

Aures habent, et non aúdient : * nares habent, et non odorábunt.

Manus habent, et non palpábunt : pedes habent, et non ambulábunt : * non clamábunt in gutture suo.

Símiles illis fiant qui fáciunt ea : * et omnes qui confídunt in eis.

Domus Israel sperávit in Dómino : * adjútor eórum et protéctor eórum est.

mouths, and they shall not speak : they have eyes, and they shall not see.

14. They have ears, and they shall not hear : they have noses, and they shall not smell.

15. They have hands and they shall not feel; they have feet, and they shall not walk : neither shall they speak through their throat.

16. Let those that make them become like unto them : and all such as put their trust in them.

17. The house of Israel hath hoped in the Lord : he is their helper and protector.

Domus Aaron sperávit in Dómino : * adjútor eórum et protéctor eórum est.

Qui timent Dóminum speravérunt in Dómino : * adjútor eórum et protector eórum est.

Dóminus memor fuit nostri : * et benedixit nobis.

Benedixit dómui Israel : * benedixit dómui Aaron.

Benedixit ómnibus qui timent Dóminum : * pusillis cum majoribus.

Adjiciat Dóminus super vos : * super vos, et super

18. The house of Aaron hath hoped in the Lord : he is their helper and protector.

19. They that fear the Lord have hoped in the Lord : he is their helper and protector.

20. The Lord hath been mindful of us : and hath blessed us.

21. He hath blessed the house of Israel: he hath blessed the house of Aaron.

22. He hath blesed all that fear the Lord : the least together with the greatest.

23. May the Lord add blessings upon you : upon you, and

filios vestros.

Benedícti vos a Dómino: * qui fecit cœlom et térram.

Cœlum cœli Dómino : * terram autem dedit filiis hóminum.

Non mortui laudábunt te, Dómine: * neque omnes qui descéndunt in inférnum.

Sed nos qui vívimus, benedícimus Dómino : * ex hoc nunc et usque in sæculum.

Gloria Patrie, & c.

Ant. Nos qui vivimus, benedícimus Dómino.

upon your children.

24. Blessed be ye of the Lord : who hath made heaven and earth.

25. The heaven of heavens is the Lord's : but the earth hath he given to the children of men.

26. The dead shall not praise thee, O Lord : neither all they that go down into hell.

27. But we who live bless the Lord: from this time forth for ever more.

Glory be to the Father, & c.

Ant. We who live, bless the Lord.

In Paschal time : — Ant. *Alleluia, alleluia, alleluia.*

In Place of the foregoing the following is frequently said.

PSALM 116. — *Laudate, Dominum.*

Laudáte Dóminum, omnes gentes: * laudade eum, omnes pópuli :

Quóniam confirmáta est super nos, misericórdia ejus * et veritas Dómini manet in æternum.

1. Praise the Lord, all ye gentiles : praise him, all ye people :

2. For his mercy is confirmed upon us : and the truth of the Lord enpureth for ever.

CAPITULUM, 2 Cor. i.

Benedictus Deus et Pater Domini nostri Jesu Christi, Pater misericordiarum, et Deus totius consolationis, qui consolatur nos in omni tribulatione nostra.

R. Deo gratias.

Blessed be the God and Father of our Lord Jesus Christ, the Father of mercies, and the God of all comfort who comforteth us in all our tribulation.

R. Thanks be to God.

SUNDAYS AND FESTIVALS. 335

Then follow the *Little Chaptre* and the *Hymn*.

HYMN.

Lucis Creator optime, Lucem dierum proferens, Primordiis lucis novæ, Mundi parans originem.	O blest Creator of the light! Who dost the dawn from darkness bring; And framing nature's depth and height; Didst with the newborn light begin.
Qui mane junctum vesperi Diem vocari præcipis: Illabitur tetrum chaos, Audi preces cum fletibus.	Who gently blending eve with morn, And morn with eve, didst call them day; Thick flows the flood of darkness down; Oh, hear us as we weep and pray!
Ne mens gravata crimine, Vitæ sit exul munere, Dum nil perenne cogitat, Seseque culpis illigat,	Keep thou our souls from schemes of crime; Nor guilt remorseful let them know; Nor thinking out on things of time, Into eternal darkness go.

Cœleste pulset ostium :
Vitale tollat præmium :
Vitemus omne noxium :
Purgemus omne possimum.

Præsta, Pater piissime,
Patrique compar Unice,
Cum Spiritu Paraclito,
Regnans per omne sæculum.
Amen.

Teach us to knock at heaven's high door;
Teach us the prize of life to win :
Teach us all evil to abhor,
And purify ourselves within,

Father of mercies ! hear our cry ;
Hear us, O sole-begotten Son !
Who, with the Holy Ghost most high,
Reignest while endles ages run.
Amen.

After which is said, with its proper Antiphon:
The *Manificat*, or *Canticle of the Blessed Virgin.*

Magnificat : * ánima mea Dominum.
Et exultávit spiritus meus : * in Deo salutári meo.
Quia respéxit humilitátem ancillæ

1. My soul doth magnify : the Lord.
2. And my spirit hath rejoiced : in God my Saviour.
3. For he hath regarded the humility

suæ : * ecce enim ex hoc beátem me dicent omnes generatiónes.

Quia fecit mihi magna qui potens est : * et sanctum nomen ejus.

Et misericórdia ejus a progénie in progenies: * timéntibus eum.

Fecit potentiam in bráchio suo : * dispérsit supérbos mente cordis sui.

Depósuit poténtes de sede : * et exaltávit húmiles.

Esuriéntes implévit bonis * et dívi-

of his handmaid : for behold from henceforth all generations shall call me blessed.

7. For he that is mighty hath done great things unto me : and holy is his name.

5. And his mercy is from generation to generation : unto them that fear him.

6. He hath showed strength with his arm: he hath scattered the proud in the imagination of their heart.

7. He hath put down the mighty from their seat: and hath exalted the humble.

8. He hath filled the hungry with

tes dimísit inanes.

Suscépit Israel puérum suum : * recordátus misericórdiæ suæ.

Sicut locútus est ad patres nostros :* Abraham, et sémini ejus in sæcula.

Glória Patri, &c.

good things : and the rich he hath sent empty away.

9. He hath upholden his servant Israel : being mindful of his mercy.

10. As he spake unto our fathers : to Abraham and his seed for ever.

Glory be to the Father, &c.

Here follows the *Prayer*, which is different every Sunday.

Let us Pray.

Look down we beseech thee, O Lord, upon this thy congregation, for which our Lord Jesus Christ dit not hesitate to be delivered into the hands of sinners, and to undergo the torments of the Cross: who liveth and reigneth whith thee, in the unity of the Holy Ghost, one God, world without end. Amen.

V. Benedicámus Dómino.

R. Deo grátias.

V. Fidelium ánimæ per misericórdiam Dei requiéscant in pace.

R. Amen.

V. Let us bless the Lord.

R. Thanks be to God.

V. May the souls of the faithful, through the mercy of God, rest in peace.

R. Amen.

Here follows the *Antiphon of the Blessed Virgin* proper for the season, if it is to be sung.

I.

From Vespers of Saturday before First Sunday in Advent to the Purification, inclusive.

Alma Redemptoris Mater, quæ pervia cœli,
Porta manes, et Stella maris, succurre cadenti,
Surgere qui curat, populo : tu quæ genuisti.
Natura mirante, tuum sanctum Genitorem :

Mother of Christ ! hear thou thy people's cry,
Star of the deep, and Portal of the sky !
Mother of Him who thee from nothing made,
Sinking we strive, and call to thee for aid

Virgo prius ac posterius, Gabriëlis ab ore, Sumens illud Ave, peccatorum miserere.	Oh, by that joy which Gabriel brought to thee, Thou Virgin first and last, let us thy mercy see.

IN ADVENT.

V. Angelus Domini nuntiavit Mariæ.
R. Et concepit de Spiritu Sancto.

V. The angel of the Lord announce l unto Mary.
R. And she conceived of the Holy Ghost.

Oremus.

Let us Pray.

Gratiam tuam quæsumus Domine, mentibus nostris infunde; ut qui, angelo nuntiante, Christi Filii tui incarnationem cognovimus, per passionem ejus et crucem ad resurrectionis gloriam perducamur. Per

Pour forth, we beseech thee, O Lord, thy grace into our hearts; that we, to whom the incarnation of Christ thy Son was made known by the message of an angel, may by his passion and cross, be

SUNDAYS AND FESTIVALS. 341

eumdem Christum Dominum nostrum.

R. Amen.

brought to the glory of his resurrection. Through the same Christ our Lord.

R. Amen.

FROM CHRISTMAS DAY TO THE PURIFICATION.

V. Post partum virgo inviolata permansisti.
R. Dei Genitrix, intercede pro nobis.

V. After childbirth thou didst remain a pure virgin.
R. Intercede for us, O Mother of God.

Oremus.

Deus, qui salutis æternæ, beatæ Mariæ virginitate fecunda, humano generi præmia præstitisti; tribue, quæsumus, ut ipsam pro nobis intercedere sentiamus, per quam meruimus auctorem vitæ suscipere Do-

Let us Pray.

O God, who, by the fruitful virginity of blessed Mary, hast given to mankind the rewards of eternal salvation ; grant, we beseech thee, that we may experience her intercession for us, through whom we

minum nostrum Jesum Christum Filium tuum. Qui vivit, &c.

R. Amen.
V. Divinum auxilium maneat semper nobiscum.
R. Amen.
Pater noster (*secreto.*)

have deserved to receive the author of life, our Lord Jesus Christ thy Son. Who liveth, &c.

R. Amen.
V. May the divine assistance remain always with us.
R. Amen.
Our Father, (*secretly.*)

II.

From Compline on the Feast of the Purification to Maunday-Thursday, exclusively.

Ave, Regina cœlorum !
Ave, domina angelorum !
Salve, radix, salve porta,
Ex qua mundo Lux est orta.

Gaude, Virgo gloriosa,

Hail, O Queen of Heaven enthron'd !
Hail, by angel's mistress own'd !
Root of Jesse, Gate of morn,
Whence the world's true light was born.

Glorious Virgin joy to thee,

SUNDAYS AND FESTIVALS. 343

Super omnes speciosa,	Loveliest whom in Heaven they see.
Vale, O valde decora!	Fairest thou where all are fair!
Et pro nobis Christum exora!	Plead with Christ our sins to spare.

V. Dignare me laudare te, Virgo sacrata.
R. Da mihi virtutem contra hostes tuos.

V. Vouchsafe that I may praise thee, O sacred Virgin.
R. Give me strength against, thine enemies.

Oremus.

Let us Pray.

Concede, misericors Deus, fragilitati nostræ præsidium ; ut qui sanctæ Dei Genitricis memoriam agimus, intercessionis ejus auxilio a nostris iniquitatibus resurgamus. Per eumdem Christum, &c.
R. Amen.

Grant, O merciful God, support to our frailty ; that we who commemorate the holy Mother of God, may, by the help of her intercession, arise from our iniquities. Through the same Christ our Lord, &c.
R. Amen.

℣. Divinum auxilium maneat semper nobiscum.
℟. Amen.

℣. May the divine assistance remain always with us.
℟. Amen.

III.
From Compline on Holy Saturday till Trinity eve.

Regina Cœli, lætare! alleluia.
Quia quem meruisti portare; alleluia.

Resurrexit sicut dixit; alleluia.
Ora pro nobis Deum; alleluia.
℣. Gaude et lætare, Virgo Maria: alleluia.
℟. Quia surrexit Dominus vere: alleluia.

Joy to thee, O Queen of Heaven! alleluia.
He whom thou wast meet to bear; alleluia.

As he promis'd hath arisen; alleluia.
Pour for us to him thy prayer; alleluia.
℣. Rejoice and be glad, O Virgin Mary; alleluia.
℟. For the Lord hath risen indeed; alleluia.

Oremus.

Deus, qui per resurrectionem Filii

Let us Pray.

O God, who didst vouchsafe to give

SUNDAYS AND FESTIVALS. 345

tui Domini nostri Jesu Christi mundum lætificare dignatus es ; præsta, quæsumus, ut per ejus Genitricem Virginem Mariam perpetuæ capiamus gaudia vitæ. Per eumdem Christum, &c.

R. Amen.
V. Divinum auxilium maneat semper nobiscum.
R. Amen

joy to the world through the resurrection of thy Son, our Lord Jesus Christ ; grant we beseech thee, that, through his Mother, the Virgin Mary we may obtain the joys of everlasting life. Through the same Christ, &c.

R. Amen.
V. May the divine assistance remain always with us.
R. Amen.

IV.

From First Vespers of Trinity Sunday to Advent.

Salve, Regina, mater misericordiæ ;
Vita, dulcedo, et spes nostra, salve.

Hail, holy Queen, Mother of Mercy ;
Our life, our sweetness, and our hope, all hail.

Ad te clamamus, exules filii Evæ; Ad te suspiramus, gementes et flentes in hac lacrymarum valle.

Eia ergo, Advocata nostra,

Illos tuos misericordes oculos ad nos converte;

Et Jesum, benedictum fructum ventris tui.

Nobis post hoc exilium ostende,

O clemens, O pia, O dulcis Virgo Maria.

V. Ora pro nobis, sancta Dei Genitrix.

R. Ut digni efficiamur promissionibus Christi.

Oremus.

Omnipotens, sempiterne Deus, qui gloriosæ Virginis

To thee we cry, poor banished sons of Eve; To thee we sigh, weeping and mourning in this vale of tears.

Therefore, O our Advocate,

Turn thou on us those merciful eyes of thine;

And after this our exile show us,

Jesus, the blessed fruit of thy womb,

O merciful, O kind, O sweet Virgin Mary.

V. Pray for us, O holy Mother of God.

R. That we may be made worthy of the promises of Christ.

Let us Pray.

Almighty, everlasting God, who, by the co-operation

SUNDAYS AND FESTIVALS. 347

Matris Mariæ corpus et animam, ut dignum Filii tui habitaculum effici mereretur, Spiritu Sancto co-operante, præparasti ; da ut cujus commemoratione lætamur, ejus pia intercessione ab instantibus malis et a morte perpetua liberemur. Per eumdem Christum, &c.

R. Amen.
V. Divinum auxilium maneat semper nobiscum.
R. Amen.

of the Holy Ghost, didst prepare the body and soul of Mary, glorious Virgin and Mother, to become the worthy habitation of thy Son ; grant that we may be delivered from instant evils and from everlasting death by her gracious intercession, in whose commemoration we rejoice. Through the same Christ, &c.

R. Amen.
V. May the divine assistance remain always with us.
R. Amen.

CONCLUDING PRAYER.

To the most Holy and undivided Trinity, to the crucified humanity of our Lord

Jesus Christ, to the most blessed and glorious and ever-faithful virginity of the Virgin Mary, and to the assembly of all the Saints in heaven, may everlasting praise, honor, power and glory be given, by every creature, and to us, also, the remission of all our sins, through never ending ages. Amen.

V. Blessed be the womb of the Virgin Mary, which bore the Son of the eternal Father!

R. And blesssd be the breasts which nourished Christ our Lord.

Our Father, *and* Hail Mary.

THE BENEDICTION OF
THE MOST HOLY SACRAMENT.

When the Priest opens the Tabernacle, and incenses the Blessed Sacrament, is sung, the Hymn. *O Salutaris hostia.*

HYMN.

O salutaris hostia,	O saving Victim! opening wide
Quæ cœli pandis ostium:	The gate of heaven to man below!

SUNDAYS AND FESTIVALS.

Bella premunt hostilia,	Our foes press on from every side;
Da robur, fer auxilium.	Thine aid supply, thy strength bestow.
Uni trinoque Domino	To thy great name be endless praise,
Sit sempiterna gloria!	Immortal Godhead, one in three!
Qui vitam sine termino	Oh, grant us endless length of days
Nobis donet in patria.	In our true native land with thee!
Amen.	Amen.

After which follows the *Litany of the Blessed Virgin*, p. 52, or some Psalms, or Antiphon, or Hymn appropriate to the Feast, or in honor of the Most Holy Sacrament. Here also are recited the corresponding Versicles and Prayers, as also any Prayer enjoined by the Bishop.

Then is sung the Hymn, *Tantum ergo Sacramentum*, all present making a profound inclination (not prostration) while the words *Veneremur cernui* are being said.

HYMN.

Pange lingua gloriosi	Sing, my tongue, the Saviour's glory
Corporis mysterium,	Of his flesh the mystery sing;

| Sanguinisque preti-
osi,
Quem in mundi pre-
tium,
Fructus ventris gene-
rosi
Rex effudit gentium, | Of the Blood, all price
exceeding,
Shed by our immor-
tal King,
Destined for the
world's redemption,
From a noble womb
to spring. |

Nobis datus, nobis natus
Ex intacta Virgine,

Et in mundo conver-
satus,
Sparso verbi semine,

Sui moras incolatus

Miro clausit ordine.

Of a pure and spot-
less Virgin
Born for us on earth
below,
He, as man with man
conversing,
Stayed, the seeds of
truth to sow ;
Then he closed in so-
lemn order
Wondrously his life
of woe.

In supremæ nocte
cœnæ,
Recumbens cum fratri-
bus,
Observata lege plene

Cibis in legalibus,

On the night of that
Last supper,
Seated with his
chosen band,
He the paschal victim
eating,
First fulfils the law's
command ;

MOST HOLY SACRAMENT.

Cibum turbæ duodenæ Se dat suis manibus.	Then, as food to all his brethren, Gives himself with his own hand.
Verbum caro, panem verum Verbo carnem efficit : Fitque Sanguis Christi merum : Et si sensus deficit Ad firmandum cor sincerum Sola fides sufficit.	Word made flesch, the bread of nature By his word to flesh he turns : Wine into his blood he changes : What though sense no change discerns? Only be the heart in earnest, Faith her lesson quickly learns,
Tantum ergo Sacramentum. Veneremur cernui : Et antiquum documentum Novo cedat ritui : Præstet fides supplementum Sensuum defectui.	Down in adoration falling, Lo ! the sacred host we hail ; Lo ! o'er ancient forms departing, Newer rites of grace prevail ! Faith, for all defects supplying, Where thee feeble senses fail.

Genitori, Genitoque
Laus et jubilatio,
Salus, honor, virtus quoque
Sit et benedictio :

Procedenti ab utroque

Compar sit laudatio.

To the everlasting Father,
And the Son who reigns on high,
With the Holy Ghost proceeding,
Forth from each eternally,
Be salvation, honor, blessing,
Might, and endless majesty.

To which succeed the following *Versicle* and *Prayer* :

V. Panem de cœlo prestitisti eis. [Alleluia.]

R. Omne delecta mentum in se habentem. [Alleluia.]

V. Thou didst give them bread from heaven. [Alleluia.]

R. Containing in itself all sweetness. [Alleluia.]

Alleluia is said in Paschal time, and during the Octave of *Corpus Christi*.

Oremus.

Deus, qui nobis sub sacramento mi-

Let us Pray.

O God, who, in this wonderful Sa-

rabili Passionis tuæ memoriam reliquisti; tribue, quæsumus, ita nos Corporis et Sanguinis tui sacra mysteria venerari, ut redemptionis tuo fructum in nobis jugiter sentiamus. Qui vivis et regnas in sæcula sæculorum. Amen.

crament has left us a memorial of thy Passion; grant, we beseech thee, that we may so worthily reverence the sacred mysteries of thy Body and Blood, that we may continually find in our souls the fruit of thy redemption. Who livest and reignest for ever and ever. Amen.

When the Priest gives the benediction with he Blessed Sacrament, bow down and profoundly adore your Saviour there present ; give him thanks for all his mercies, offer your whole self to him, to be his for ever ; and earnestly beg his blessing upon you and yours, and upon his whole Church. Or you may say a hymn to the Blessed Sacrament.

Hymns.

Whitsun-tide.
(For the Sodality.)

Veni Creator Spiritus,	Come, O Creator Spirit blest!
Mentes tuorum visita,	And in our souls take up thy rest;
Imple superna gratia,	Come, with thy grace and heavenly aid,
Quæ tu creasti pectora.	To fill the heart which thou hast made.
Qui diceris Paraclitus,	Great Paraclete! to thee we cry,
Altissimi donum Dei,	O highest gift of God most high!
Fons vivus, ignis, charitas,	O fount of live! O fire of love!
Et spiritalis unctio.	And sweet anointing from above.
Tu septiformis munere,	Thou in thy sevenfold gifts art known:
Digitus Paternæ dexteræ,	The finger of God's hand we own.

Tu rite promissum Patris,
Sermonis ditans guttura.

Accende lumen sensibus,
Infunde amorem cordibus,
Infirma nostri corporis
Virtute firmans perpeti.

Hostem repellas longius,
Pacemque dones protinus;
Ductore sic te prævio
Vitemus omne noxium.

Per te sciamus da Patrem,
Noscamus atque Filium,
Teque utriusque Spiritum,
Credamus omni tempore.

The promise of the Father thou!
Who dost the tongue with pow'r endow,

Kindle our senses from above,
And make our hearts o'erflow with love,
With patience firm, and virtue high,
The weakness of our flesh supply.

Far from us drive the foe we dread,
And grant us thy true peace instead:
So shall we not, with thee for guide.
Turn from the path of life aside.

Oh, may thy grace on us bestow,
The Father and the Son to know,
And thee through endless timed confess'd
Of both the eternal Spirit blest.

HYMNS.

Deo Patri sit gloria,
Et Filio, qui a mortuis.
Surrexit, ac Paraclito,
In sæculorum sæcula.

Amen.

All glory while the ages run
Be to the Father and the Son
Who rose from death; the same to thee,
O Holy Ghost, eternally.

Amen.

Hymn of the Blessed Virgin Mary.
(For the Sodality.

Ave maris stella,
Dei Mater alma,
Atque Semper Virgo,
Felix cœli porta.

Gentle Star of ocean!
Portal of the sky!
Ever Virgin Mother
Of the Lord most high!

Sumens illud Ave
Gabrielis ore,
Funda nos in pace,
Mutans Evæ nomen.

Oh! by Gabriel's Ave,
Utterred long ago,
Eva's name reversing,
Stablish peace below.

Solve vincla reis,
Profer lumen cæsis,
Mala nostra pelle,
Bona cuncta posce.

Break the captive's fetters,
Light on blindness pour;
All our ills expelling,
Every bliss implore.

Monstra te esse Matrem, Sumat per te preces, Qui pro nobis natus, Tulit esse tuus.	Show thyself a Mother, Offer him our sighs Who for us incarnate, Did not thee dispise.
Virgo singularis, Inter omnes mitis, Nos culpis solutos, Mites fac et castos.	Virgin of all virgins! To thy shelter take ns : Gentlost of the gentle! Chaste and gentle make us.
Vitam præsta puram, Iter para tutum; Ut videntus Jesum, Semper collætemur.	Still, as on we journey, Help our weak endeavor; Till with thee and Jesus, We rejoice forever.
Sit laus Deo Patri, Summo Christo decus, Spiritui Sancto, Tribus honor unus.	Through the highest heaven, To the Almighty Three, Father, Son, and Spirit One same glory be.
Amen.	Amen.

Hymn

To the Honor of Mary, the Virgin Mother of God. Composed by St. Casimir.

(New Translation.)

DECAS I.	DECADE I.

Omni die dic Mariæ
Mea laudes anima ;
Ejus festa, ejus gesta
Cole devotissima.
	Each day, my soul,
	  Tell Mary's praise,
	Her ev'ry deed,
	  Her Festal days.

Contemplare et mirare
Ejus celsitudinem,
Dic felicem Genitricem,
Dic beatam Virginem.
	With wond'ring look,
	  Come contemplate
	Her Mother's joy,
	  Blest Virgin state!

Ipsam cole, ut de mole
Criminum te liberet,
Hanc appella, ne procella
Vitiorum superet.
	Oh, call on Her,
	  Soon thus to be
	From weight of sin
	  And tempest free!

Hæc persona nobis dona
Contulit cœlestia.
Hæc Regina nos divinâ
Collustravit gratiâ.
	Us She endows
	  With heav'nly gifts;
	With grace to shine,
	  Our heart uplifts.

Lingua mea, dic trophæ,
Virginis puerpuræ.
Que inflictum maledictum
Miro transfert germine.

Sine fine dic Reginæ
Mundi laudum cantica;
Ejus bona semper sona,
Semper illa prædica.

Omnes mei sensus ei
Personate gloriam.
Frequentate tam beatæ
Virginis memoriam.

Nullus certè tam disertæ,
Exstat eloquentiæ,
Qui condignos promat hymnos
Ejus excellentiæ.

Omnes laudent, undè gaudent,
Matrem Dei Virginem,
Nullus fingat quod attingat
Ejus celestudinem.

Thy meed, my tongue,
Accomplish well,
Of curse removed,
Her trophies tell.

Earth's Queen is She—
Thy whole life long,
Proclaim Her praise
In ceaseless song!

With it resound
My senses all;
So blest a Maid
Oft-times recall!

Not one there is
Of eloquence
Meet to declare
Her excellence!

Praise, all, your Joy,
God's Mother maid
By none 't will be
With truth portrayed;

Sed necesse, quod prodesse
Piis constat mentibus.
Ut intendam, quod impendam
In ipsius laudibus.
    Ave Maria.

Still, In Her praise.
My thouhgt imparts
Some benefit
To holy hearts.
    Hail Mary.

DECAS II.

Quamvis sciam, quod Mariam
Nemo dignè prædicet,
Tamen vanus et insanus
Quisquis illam reticet.

DECADE II.

Though none I know
To praise Her meet,
'Twould madness be
Her not to greet.

Cujus vita erudita
Disciplina cœlica;
Argumenta et figmenta
Destruxit hæretica.

With thinghs of Heav'n
Her learning fraught,
False dreams of men
Hath put to nought.

Cujus mores tamquam flores
Exornant Ecclesiam;
Actiones et sermones
Miram præstant gratiam.

Her life the Church
Bedecks, like flowers;
Her words and deeds
Are grace's dow'rs.

Evæ crimen nobis limen
Paradisi clauserat.

Eve's sin to us
Closed Paradise

Hæc dum credit et obedit, Cœli claustra reserat.	To Mary's faith It open flies.
Propter Evam homo sævam Accepit sententiam ; Per Mariam habet viam Quæ ducit ad patriam.	Lost man, by Eve, Hath exile found : By Mary he Is homeward bound.
Hæc manda et laudanda Cunctis specialiter: Venerari, prædicari Eam decet jugiter.	The praise of all Her merit gains, And specially Their love obtains.
Ipsa donet, ut, quod monet Natus ejus, faciam : Ut finita carnis vita Lætus hunc aspiciam.	Her Son, obey'd Through Her, may I Behold with joy Whene'er I die !
Ocuntarum fœminarum Decus atque gloria ! Quam electam et evectam Scimus super omnia.	O'er women blest,— Their glory, Thou ! How high o'er all We the avow !
Clemens audi,tuæ laudi Quos instantes conspicis,	Hear graciously, And save from Hell,

Munda reos, et fac eos
Donis dignos colicis

Make meet for grace
Who praise Thee well.

Virgo Jesse, spes op-
pressæ
Mentis et refugium,
Decus mundi, lux pro-
fundi,
Domini sacrarium.
    Ave Maria.

Hope of th' opprest !
Fair Jesse's Rod !
Light of the Deep !
The Shrine of God !
Hail Mary.

DECAS III.
Vitæ forma, morum
norma,
Plenitudo gratiæ.
Dei templum, et exem-
plum
Totius justitiæ.

DECADE III.
Fulness of grace,
Life's Standard true.
God's Temple, and
Truth's Pattern new !

Virgo salve, per quam
valvæ
Cœli patent miseris;
Quam non flexit nec
allexit
Fraus serpentis veteris.

Thou to lorn souls
Dost Heav'n assure,
Nor bent nor bought
By Serpent's lure.

Generosa et formosa,
David regis filia.
Quam elegit rex, qui
regit
Et creavit omnia.

The King's fair choice,
Hail, queenly Maid
Who made all worlds.
By all obey'd.

Gemma, decens, rosa recéns,
Castitatis lilium,
Castum chorum ad polorum
Quæ perducis gaudium.

Actionis et sermonis
Facultatem tribue
Ut tuorum meritorum,
Laudes promam strenue.

Opto nimis, ut imprimis
Des mihi memoriam,
Ut decenter et frequenter
Tuam cantem gloriam.

Quamvis muta et polluta
Mea sciam labia,
Præsumendum, nec silendum
Est de tua gloria.

Virgo gaude, omni laude
Digna et præconio.

Chaste Lily flow'r!
Pure budding Rose!
Chaste choirs thou guid'st
To Heaven's repose!

Give me the pow'r
Of hand and speech,
Thy merits high
With might to preach!

But oh, to me
First mem'ry grant,
Oft as is meet,
Thy praise to chant!

Though soil'd and dumb
My lips I know,
Still I must dare
Thy meed to show.

Virgin rejoice,
Thus praised te be

Quæ damnatis liberta-
 tis
Facta es occasio.

Semper munda et fæ-
 cunda,
Virgo tu puerpera.
Mater alma velut pal-
 ma
Florens et fructifera.

Ejus flore et adore
Recreari capimus,
Cujus fructu nos a
 luctu
Liberari credimus.
  Ave Maria.

Cause to the lost
 Of liberty!

O Mother-Maid!
 O Mother pure!
Like fruitful palm,
 Aye to endure!

By Thee, sweet Flow'r
 Refresh'd to be,
We trust, whose Fruit
 Hath set us free!
  Hail Mary.

DECAS IV.

Pulchra tota sine
 notâ
Cujus cunque maculæ,
Fac nos mundos et ju-
 cundos
Te laudare sedule.

O beata, per quem
 data
Nova mundo gaudia!
Et aperta fide certa
Regna sunt cælestia.

DECADE IV.

All beauteous One
 Who know'st no stain
Oh, make us pure,
 To praise Thee fain!

By Thee, O Blest!
 Through faith, are
 given,
And op'd to men
 The realms of Heaven.

HYMNS.

Per te mundus lætabundus
Novo fulget lumine,
Antiquarum tenebrarum
Exutus caligine.
	Lo, the glad world
	   New light displays
	The darkness doff'd
	   Of ancient days.

Nunc potentas sunt egentes,
Sicut olim dixeras;
Et egeni fiunt pleni.
Ut tu prophetaveras.
	Poor are the great,
	   And rich the poor;
	As thou foretold'st,—
	   They want no more!

Per te morum corruptorum
Delinquuntur devia,
Doctrinarum perversarum
Pulsa sunt præstigia.
	Through thee the bad
	   Forsake their way;
	And doctrines strange
	   Are driven away.

Mundi luxus atque fluxus
Docuisti spernere :
Deum quæri, carnem
Vitiis resistere. (teri.
	Thou teachest us
	   The world t' eschew
	To fight with sin,
	   The flesh subdue.

Mentis cursum tendi sursum
Pietatis studio,
Corpus angi motus frangi
Pro cœlesti præmio.
	With holy zeal
	   Aloft to rise,
	The body tame,
	   For Heav'nly prize.

Tu portasti inter casti
Ventris claustra Domi-
    num
Redemptoram, ad ho
    norem
Nos reformans pristi-
    num.

Mater facta sed intacta
Genuisti filium,
Regem regum atque
    rerum
Creatorum omnium.

Benedicta, per quam
    victa
Mortis est sententia :
Destitutis spe salutis
Datur indulgentia.
    Ave Maria.

DECAS V.

Benedictus rex invictus
Cujus mater credens,
Nobis datus, ex te na-
    tus
Nostris salus generis.

Reparatrix, Consola-
    trix
Des perantis animæ

The Lord was borne
    Thy womb within,
Us to remould,
    Debased by sin.

Mother Intact
    He made all things,
Who is thy Son, —
    The King of kings!

Blest Conqu'ress, thus
    With Death to cope,
And life restore
    To sinking Hope!
        Hail Mary.

DECADE V.

Blest be the King,
    Thy conqu'ring Son,
Whose Birth for Hea-
    ven
Our race hath won!

Consoler Thou
    Of our despair

A pressura, que ventura
Malis est nos redime.

Pro me pete, ut quiete
Sempiterna perfruar,
Ne tormentis comburentis
Stagni miser obruar.

Quod requiro, quod suspiro,
Mea sana vulnera;
Et da menti te poscenti
Gratiarum munera.

Ut sim castus et modestus.
Dulcis, blandus, sobri-
Pius, rectus, circumspectus, [us,
Simultatis nescius.

Eruditus et minitus
Divinis eloquiis,
Timoratus et ornatus
Sacris exercitiis.

Constans gravis et suavis,
Benignus, amabilis

Redeem our loss,
Our ills repair!

The e'erlasting Rest,
For me obtain,
Saved from the Lake
Of fiery pain.

I sigh for Thee
My wounds to cure,
To my request
All grace procure!

Chaste, pure, and meek
That I may be,
Just, upright, good,
From malice free.

Of learning fraught
With holy store,
Made eloquent
In Sacred love,

Kind, grave, and firm,
In love mature,

Simplex, purus et maturus,
Patiens et humilis.

Corde prudens, ore studens,
Veritatem dicere,
Malum, nolens, Deum colens
Pio semper opere.

Esto tutrix et adjutrix —
Christiani populi;
Pacem præsta, ne molesta
Nos perturbent sæculi.

Salutaris stella maris
Summis digna laudibus,
Quæ præcellis cunctis stellis
Atque luminaribus.
    Ave Maria.

Humble, patient,
Simple, and pure.

To ill not prone,
In heart e'er wise,
Oft doing good,
Abhoring lies.

Christ's faithful souls
Aid and protect,
'Mid earthly cares
To stand erect.

Nor light nor star,
Star of the Sea,
May seek to vie
In praise with Ehee.
    Hail Mary.

HYMNS.

DECAS VI.

Tuâ dulci prece fulci
Supplices et refove,
Quidquid gravat vel
    depravat
Montes nostras, re-
move.

Virgo gaude, quod de
    fraude,
Dæmonis nos liberas,
Dum in verâ et sin-
    cerâ
Deum carne generas,

Illibata et dotata
Cœlesti progenie,
Gravidata, nec privata
Flore pudicitiæ.

Nam quod eras, per-
    severas,
Dum intacta generas,
Illum tractans atque
Per lactans,
Per quem facta fueras.

DECADE VI.

Thy sons uphold
  By thy sweet pray'r,
Their sorrows heal,
  Their guilt repair.

Glad, them to free
  From Satan's traud,
Who in true flesh
  Hast borne thy God!

With Son divine,
  How chaste a flow'r,
Retaining still
  Thy Virgin's dow'r!

A Mother, yet
  Maid undefiled
Thy Maker's nurse,
And He thy Child!

Commendare me dignare
Christo tuo Filio :
Ut non cadam, sed evadam
De mundi naufragio.

Oh, keep me near
 To Jesu's side!
Tho' wrecked the world,
 Still safe I'll ride.

Fac me mitem, pelle litem,
Compesce lasciviam,
Contrà crimen da munimen
Et mentis constantiam.

Rein in my wrath,
 Drive lust away
When sin allures,
 Be Thou my stay.

Non me liget, nec fatiget
Sæculi cupiditas :
Que indurat et obscarat
Mentes sibi subditas.

No wordly aim
 My soul deprave ;
Grows blind and hard,
 Ambition's slave!

Nunquàm ira, nunquàm dira
Me vincat elatio :
Que multorum fit malorum,
Frequentur occasio

Nor pride, nor wrath
 My bosom swell;
Where triumph these,
 Who hath not fell?

Ora Deum ut cor meum Sua servet gratia ; Nec antiquus inimicus Seminet zizania.	Pray God, by grace, My heart to keep ; Lest Satan sow Tares while I sleep.
Da levamen et juvamen Tuum illis jugiter, Tua festa sive gesta Qui colunt alacriter. Ave Maria.	Aid and console, Who love to praise Thy deeds divine, Thy Festal Days ! Hail Mary.

Fourth Hymn for the Sodality.

Tantum ergo Sacramentum.

(See page 349.)

Adeste Fideles.

Adeste fideles,
Læti triumphantes;
Venite, venite in Bethlehem
Natum videte
Regem angelorum :
Venite adoremus,
Venite adoremus,
Venite adoremus Dominum.

Deum de Deo,
Lumen de lumine,
Gestant puellæ viscera
Deum verum,
Genitum, non factum :
   Venite adoremus, etc.

Cantet nunc Io!
Chorus angelorum :
Cantet nunc aula cælestium,
Gloria
In excelsis Deo!
   Venite adoremus, etc.

Ergo qui natus
Die hodierna,
Jesu tibi sit gloria :
Patris æterni
Verbo caro factum !
   Venite adoremus, etc.

Adeste Fideles.

Ye faithful, approach ye,
Joyfully triumphing :
Oh, come ye, oh, come ye, to Bethlehem :
Come and behold ye
Born the King of angels :
Oh, come, let us worship.
Oh, come, let us worship,
Oh, come, let us worship Christ the Lord.

True God of God,
True Light of Light,
Lo, He disdains not the Virgins womb ;
Very God
Begotten, not created ;
Oh, come, let us, worship, &c.

Sing Halleluiah,
Let the courts of Heaven
Ring with the Angel-chorus—
Praise the Lord,
Glory to God in the highest :
Oh, come, let us, worship, &c.

Yea, Lord, we greet thee,
Born this happy morning ;
Jesu, to thee be glory giv'n :
Word of the Father
In our flesh appearing :
Oh, come, let us worship, &c.

Sequence.

Veni Sancte Spiritus,
Et emitte cœlitus
  Lucis tuæ radium :

Veni pater pauperum
Veni dator munerum,
  Veni lumen cordium.

Consolator optime,
Dulcis hospes animæ,
  Dulce refrigerium.

In labore requies,
In æstu temperies,
  In fletu solatium.

O lux beatissima,
Reple cordis intima
  Tuorum fidelium.

Sine tuo nomine,
Nihil est in homine,
  Nihil est innexium.

Lava quod est sordidum
Rige quod est aridum :
  Sana quod est saucium.

Sequence.

Holy Spirit! Lord of light!
From thy clear celestial height,
   Thy pure beaming radiance give

Come, thou father of the poor!
Come with treasures which endure!
   Come, thou light of all that live.

Thou, of all consolers best,
Visiting the troubled breast,
   Dost refreshing peace bestow;

Thou in toil art comfort sweet
Pleasant coolness in the heat;
   Solace in the midst of woe.

Light immortal! light divine!
Visit thou these hearts of thine,
   And our inmost being fill

If thou take thy grace away,
Nothing pure in man will stay;
   All is good is turned to ill.

Heal our wounds—our strength renew
On our dryness pour thy dew;
   Wash the stains of guilt away;

Flecte quod est rigidum;
Fove quod est frigidum;
  Rege quod est devium.

Da tuis fidelibus
In te confidentibus
  Sacrum septenarium.

Da virtutis meritum :
Da salutis exitum :
  Da perenne gaudium.
              Amen.

Hyms of the Blessed Sacrament.

Verbum supernum prodiens,
Nec Patris linquens dexteram,
Ad opus suum exiens,
Venit ad vitæ vesperam.

In mortem a discipulo
Suis tradendus æmulis,
Prius in vitæ ferculo
Se tradidit discipulis.

Quibus sub bina specie
Carnem dedit et sanguinem,
Ut duplicis substantiæ
Totum cibaret honinem.

Rend the stubborn heart and will;
Melt the frozen, warm the chill;
 Guide the steps that go astray.

Thou, on those who evermore
Thee confess and thee adore,
 In thy sevenfold gifts descend:

Give them comfort when they die;
Give them life with thee on high;
Give them joys which never end.
                              Amen.

Hymns of the Blessed Sacrament.

The Word, descending from above,
 Through with the Father still on high,
Went forth upon his work of love,
 And soon to life's last eve drew nigh.

He shortly to a death accursed
 By a disciple shall be given;
But, to his twelve disciples, first
 He gives, himself, the bread from heaven.

Himself in either kind he gave;
 He gave his flesh, he gave his blood;
Of flesh and blood all men are made;
 And he of man would be the food.

Se nascens dedit socium,
Convescens in edulium,
Se moriens in pretium,
Se regnans dat in præmium.

O salutaris Hostia,
Quæ cœli pandis ostium,
Bella premunt hostilia,
Da robur, fer auxilium.

Uni trinoque Domino
Sit sempiterna gloria.
Qui vitam sine termino
Nobis donet in patria.
                    Amen.

Prose.

Ave verum Corpus, natum
  Ex Maria virgine,
Vere passum, immolatum,
  In cruce pro homine.

Cujus latus perforatum
  Vero fluxit sanguine,
Esto nobis prægustatum,
  Mortis in examine.

O clemens, O pie,
O dulcis Jesu, Fili Mariæ.

HYMNS.

At birth, our brother he became;
  At board, himself as food he gives;
To ransom us he died in shame;
  As our reward, in bliss he lives.

O saving Victim! opening wide
  The gate of heaven to man below!
Our foes press on from every side;
  Thine aid supply, thy strength bestow.

To thy great name be endless praise,
  Immortal Godhead, one in three!
Oh, grant us endless length of days
  In our true native land with thee!
                                Amen.

Prose.

Hail to thee! true Body, sprung
From the Virgin Mary's womb!
The same that on the cross was hung,
And bore for man the bitter doom!

Thou, whose side was pierced, and flow'd,
Both with wather and with blood;
Suffer us to taste of thee,
In our life's last agony.

O kind, O loving One!
O sweet Jesu, Mary's Son!

THE
Dolors of the Blessed Virgin Mary.

Stabat Mater dolorosa,
Justa crucem lacrymosa,
  Dum pendebat Filius.
Cujus animam gementem,
Contristatum, et dolentem,
  Pertransivit gladius.

O quam tristis et afflicta
Fuit illa benedicta
  Mater Unigeniti!
Quæ mœrebat, et dolebat,
Pia Mater dum videbat
  Nati pœnas inclyti.

Quis est homo, qui non fleret,
Matrem Christi si videre
  In tanto supplicio?
Quis non posset contristari,
Christi Matrem contemplari
  Dolentem cum Filio?

Pro peccatis suæ gentis,
Vidit Jesum in tormentis,
  Et flagellis subditum.
Vidit suum dulcem natum
Moriendo, desolatum,
Dum emisit spiritum,

THE
Dolors of the Blessed Virgin Mary.

At the cross her station keeping,
Stood the mournful mother weeping,
   Close to Jesus to the last :
Through her heart, his sorrow sharing,
All his bitter anguish wearing,
   Now at length the sword had passed.

Oh, how sad and sore distressed
Was that mother highly blest
   Of the sole begotten One!
Christ above in torment hangs;
She beneath beholds the pangs
   Of her dying glorious Son.

Is there one who would not weep
Whelmed in miseries so deep
   Christ's dear mother to behold!
Can the human heart refrain
From partaking in her pain,
   In that mother's pain untold!

Bruised, derided, cursed, defiled,
She beheld her tender child
   All with bloody scourges rent.
For the sins of his own nation
Saw him hang in desolation,
   Till his spirit forth he sent.

Eia Mater, fons amoris,
Me sentire vim doloris
  Fac, ut tecum lugeam.
Fac ut ardeat cor meum
In amando Christum Deum,
  Ut sibi complaceam.

Sancta Mater, istud agas,
Crucifixi fige plagas
  Cordi meo valide.
Tui Nati vulnerati,
Tam dignati pro me pati,
Pœnas mecum divide.

Fac me tecum pie liere,
Crucifixi condolere,
Donec ego vixero.
Juxta crucem tecum stare,
Et me tibi sociare,
  In planctu desidero.

Virgo virginum præclara,
Mihi jam non sis amara,
  Fac me tecum plangere.
Fac ut portem Christi mortem
Passionis fac consortem
Et plagas recolere.

Fac me plagis vulnerari,
Fac me cruce inebriari,
  Et cruore filii.

O thou mother! font of love
Touch my spirit from above,
　Make my heart with thine accord :
Make me feel as thou hast felt;
Make my soul to glow and melt
　With the love of Christ my Lord.

Holy mother! pierce me through :
In my heart each wound renew
　Of my Saviour crucified :
Let me share with thee his pain,
Who for all my sins was slain,
　Who for me in torments died.

Let me mingle tears with thee,
Mourning him who mourned for me,
　All the days that I may live :
By the cross with thee to stay;
There with thee to weep and pray
　Is all I ask of thee to give.

Virgin of all virgins blest!
Listen to my fond request;
　Let me share thy grief divine;
Let me, to my latest breath,
In my body bear the death
　Of that dying Son of thine.

Wounded with his every wound,
Steep my soul till it hath swooned
　In his very blood away

Flammis ne urar succensus
Per te, Virgo, sim defensus,
　In die judicii.

Christe cum sit hinc exire,
Da per Matrem me venire
　Ad palmam victoriæ.
Quando corpus morietur,
Fac ut animæ donetur
Paradisi gloria.　Amen.

Hymn for Trinity Sunday.

Jam sol recedit igneus,
Tu lux perrenis Unitas,
Nostris, beata Trinitas,
Infunde amorem cordibus.

Te mane laudum carmine,
Te deprecamur vespere;
Digneris, ut te supplicos
Laudemus inter cœlites.

Patri, simulque Filio,
Tibique Sancte Spirtus,
Sicut fuit, sit jugiter
Sæclum per omne gloria.
　　　　　　Amen.

Be to me, Virgin nigh,
Lest in flames I burn and die,
  In his awful judgment-day.

Christ, when thou shalt call me hence,
Be thy mother my defence,
  Be thy cross my victory;
While my body here decays,
May my soul thy goodness praise,
Safe in paradise with thee.   Amen.

Hymn for Trinity Sunday.

Now doth the fiery sun decline :—
Thou Unity Eternal ! shine ;
Thou Trinity, thy blessings pour,
And make our hearts with love run o'er.

Thee in the hymns of morn we praise ;
To thee our voice at eve we raise ;
Oh, grant us, with thy saints on high,
Thee through all time to glorify.

Praise to the Father with the Son,
And Holy Spirit, three in One;
As ever was in ages past,
And shall be so while ages last.
                            Amen.

Christmas.

Jesu, Redeemer of the world!
 Who, ere the earliest dawn of light,
Wast from eternal ages born,
 Immense in glory as in might.

Immortal Hope of all mankind!
 In whom the Father's face we see;
Hear thou the prayers thy people pour,
 This day throughout the world to thee.

Remember, O Creator Lord!
 That in the Virgin's sacred womb
Thou wast conceived, and of her flesh
 Didst our mortality assume.

This ever-blest recurring-day
 Its witness bears, that all alone,
From thy own Father's bosom forth,
 To save the world thou camest down.

O day! to which the seas and sky,
 And earth and heaven, glad welcome
  sing :
O day! which healed our misery,
 And brought on earth salvation's king.

We too O Lord, who have been cleansed
 In thy own fount of blood divine,
Offer the tribute of sweet song,
 On this blest natal day of thine.

O Jesu! born of Virgin bright,
Immortal glory be to thee;
Praise to the Father infinite,
And Holy Ghost eternally.

Epiphany.

Bethlehem! of noblest cities
  None can once with thee compare
Thou alone the Lord from heaven
  Didst for us incarnate bear.

Fairer than the sun at morning
  Was the star that told his birth;
To the lands their God announcing,
  Hid beneath a form of earth.

By its lambent beauty guided,
  See, the Eastern kings appear;
See them bend, their gifts to offer—
  Gifts of incence, gold and myrrh.

Offerings of mystic meaning;—
  Incense doth the God disclose;
Gold a royal child proclaimeth;
  Myrrh a future tomb foreshows.

Holy Jesu! in thy brightness
  To the gentile world displayed!
With the Father and the Spirit,
  Endless praise to thee be paid.

The Most Holy Name of Jesus. *

Jesu ! the very thought of thee
   With sweetness fills my breast
But sweeter far thy face to see,
   And in thy presence rest.

Nor voice can sing nor heart can frame,
   Nor can the memory find,
A sweeter sound than thy blest name,
   O Saviour of mankind!

O hope of every contrite heart,
   O joy of all the meek,
To those who fall, how kind thou art!
   How good to those who seek!

But what to those who find? all this
   Nor tongue nor pen can show :
The love of Jesus, what it is,
   None but his loved ones know.

Jesu! our only joy be thou,
   As thou our prize wilt be;
Jesu! be thou our glory now,
   And through eternity.

* This is commonly called St. Bernard's Hymn.

Lent.

Thou loving Maker of mankind,
   Before thy trone we pray and weep;
Oh, strengthen us with grace divine,
   Duly this sacred Lent to keep.

Searcher of hearts! thou dost our ills
   Discern, and all our weakness know;
Again to thee with tears we turn;
   Again to us thy mercy show.

Much have we sinn'd; but we confess
   Our guilt, and all our faults deplore
Oh, for the praise of thy great name,
   Our fainting souls ta health restore.

And grant us, while by fasts we strive
   This mortal body to control,
To fast from all the food of sin,
   And so to purify the soul.

Hear us, O Trinity thrice blest!
   Sole Unity! to the we cry :
Vouchsafe us from these fasts below
   To reap immortal fruit on high.

Passion-tide.—The Holy Cross.

Forth comes the standard of the King :
   All hail, thou mystery adored !
Hail, Cross ! on which the Life himself
   Died, and by death our life restored.

On which our Saviour's holy side,
   Rent open with a cruel spear,
Of blood and water poured a stream,
   To wash us from defilement clear.

O sacred wood ! in thee fulfilled
   Was holy David's truthful lay ;
Which told the world, that from a tree
   The Lord should all the nations sway.

Most royally empurpled o'er,
   How beauteously thy stem doth shine !
How glorious was its lot to touch
   Those limbs so holy and divine !

Thrice blest, upon whose arms outstretched
   The Saviour of the world reclined;
Balance sublime ! upon whose beam
   Was weighed the ransom of mankind.

Hail, Cross ! thou only hope of man,
   Hail, on this holy Passion-day !
To saints increase the grace they have :
   From sinners purge their guilt away.

Salvation's spring, blest Trinity,
  Be praise to thee through earth and skies !
Thou through the Cross the victory
  Dost give ; oh, also give the prize !

The Crucifixion.

O'erwhelmed in depths of woe,
  Upon the tree of scorn
Hangs the Redeemer of mankind,
  Whit racking anguish torn.

See ! how the nails those hands
  And feet so tender rend ;
See ! down his face, and neck, and breast,
  His sacred blood descend.

Shall man alone be mute ?
  Come, youth ! and hoary hairs !
Come, rich and poor ! come, all mankind
  And bathe those feet in tears.

Come ! fall before his Cross,
  Who shed for us his blood ;
Who died the victim of pure love,
  To make us sons of God.

Jesu ! all praise to thee,
  Our joy and endless rest !
Be thou our guide while pilgrims here,
  Our crown amid the blest.

Easter.

Now at the Lamb's high festival
  In robes of saintly white we sing,
Through the Red Sea in safety brought
  By Jesus our immortal king.

O charity divine! his blood
  He gives to crown the royal feast;
His flesh for us he immolates,
  Himself the victim, love the priest.

And as the avenging angel passed
  Of old the blood-besprinkled door;
As the cleft sea a passage gave,
  Then closed to whelm the Egytians o'er.

So Christ our paschal sacrifice,
  Has brought us safe all perils through;
While for unleavened bread we need
  But heart sincere and purpose true.

Hail, purest Victim heaven could find,
  The powers of hell to overthrow!
Who didst the cains of death destroy:
  Who dost the prize of life bestow.

Hail, victor Christ! heil, risen King!
  To thee alone belongs the crown;
Who hast the heavenly gates unbarred,
  And dragged the prince of darkness down.

The Sacred Heart of Jesus.

All ye who seek a certain cure
   In trouble and distress,
Whatever sorrow vex the mind,
   Or guilt the soul oppress :

Jesus, who gave himself for you
   Upon the cross to die,
Opens to you his sacred heart,—
   O, to that heart draw nigh !

Ye hear how kindly he invites ;
   Ye hear his words so blest ;—
« All ye that labor, come to me,
   And I will give you rest ! »

What meeker than the Saviour's heart !—
   As on the cross he lay,
It did his murderers forgive,
   And for their pardon pray.

O heart ! thou joy of Saints on high!
   Thou hope of sinners here !
Attracted by those loving words,
   To thee I lift my prayer.

Wash thou my wounds in that dear blood
   Wich forth from thee doth flow ;
New grace, new hope inspire ; a new
   And better heart bestow.

Feast of the Annunciation.

What mortal tongue can sing thy praise.
   Dear Mother of the Lord ? —
To Angels only it belongs
   Thy glory to record.
Who born of man can penetrate
   Thy soul's majestic shrine ?
Who can thy mighty gifts unfold,
   Or rightly them divine ?
Say, Virgin, what sweet force was that,
   Which from the Father's breast
Drew forth his co-eternal Son,
   To be thy bosom's guest ?
'Twas not thy guileless faith alone,
   That lifted thee so high ;
'Twas not thy pure seraphic love,
   Or peerless chastity :
But, oh ! it was thy lowliness,
   Well pleasing to the Lord,
That made thee worthy to become
   The Mother of the Word.
Oh, loftiest !—whose humility
   So sweet it was to see !
That God, forgetful of himself,
   Abased himself to thee !
Praise to the Father, with the Son,
   And Holy Ghost, through whom
The Word eternal was conceived
   Within the Virgin's womb.

Ascension Day.

O thou eternal King most high!
  Who didst the world redeem;
And conquering death and hell, receive
  A dignity supreme.

Thou through the starry orbs, this day,
  Didst to thy throne ascend :
Thenceforth to reign in sovereign power,
  And glory without end.

There, seated in thy majesty,
  To thee submissive bow
The heav'n of heav'ns, the spacious earth,
  The depths of hell below.

With trembling there the angels see
  The changed estate of men;
The flesh which sinned, by flesh redeemed;
  Man in the Godhead reign.

There, waiting for thy faithful souls,
  Be thou to us, O Lord!
Our peerless joy while here we stay,
  In heav'n our great reward.

Renew our strength : our sins forgive;
  Our miseries efface;
And lift our souls aloft to thee,
  By thy celestial grace.

So, when thou shinest on the clouds,
  With thy angelic train,

May we be saved from vengeance due
    And our lost crowns regain.
Glory to Jesus, who returns
    Triumphantly to heaven;
Praise to the Father evermore,
    And Holy Ghost be given.

Advent.

Hark! an awful voice is sounding;
    « Christ is nigh! » it seems to say:
« Cast away the dreams of darkness,
    O ye children of the day! »
Startled at the solemn warning,
    Let the earth-bound soul arise;
Christ, her Sun, all sloth dispelling,
    Shines upon the morning skies.

Lo! the Lamb so long expected,
    Comes with pardon down from heaven:
Let us haste, with tears of sorrow,
    One and all to be forgiven.
So, when next he comes with glory,
    Wrapping all the earth in fear,
May he then as our defender
    On the clouds of heaven appear.

Honor, glory, virtue, merit,
    To the Father and the Son,
With the everlasting Spirit,
    While eternal ages run.

St. Joseph.

Joseph, pure, spouse of that immortal bride,
Who shinnes in ever-virgin glory bright,
Thy praise let all the earth reechoing send
    Back to the realms of light.

Thee, when sore doubts of thine affianced wife
Had filled thy rigtheous spirit with dismay,
An Angel visited, and, with blest words,
    Scattered they fears away.

Thine arms embraced thy Maker newly born
With him to Egypt's desert didst thou fly;
Him in Jerusalem didst seek and find :
    Oh, day of joy to thee !

Not until after death their blissful crown
Others obtain ; but unto thee was given,
In thine own lifetime to enjoy thy God,
    As do the blest in heaven.

Grant us, great Trinity, for Joseph's sake,
The heights of immortality to gain ;
There with glad tongues, thy praise to celebrate
    In one eternal strain.

All Saints.

Giver of life, eternal Lord !
    Thy own redeemed defend ;
Mother of Grace ! the children save,
    And help them the end.

Ye thousand thousand angel hosts!
  Assist us in our need;
Ye Patriarchs! with the Prophet choir!
  For our forgiveness plead.

Herald of Christ! and thou who still
  Dost heaven's dread keys retain!
Ye glorious Apostles all!
  Unloose our guilty chain.

Army of Martyrs! holy priests
  In beauteous array!
Ye happy troops of virgins chaste!
  Wash all our sins away.

All ye who high above the stars
  In heavenly glory reign!
May we through your blest prayers the gifts
  Of endless life obtain.

Praise, honor, to the Father be,
  Praise to his only Son;
Praise to the Spirit Paraclete,
  While ceaseless ages run.

St. Michael.

O Jesu! life-spring of the soul!
  The Father's power and glory bright!
Thee with the Angels we extol;
  From the they draw their life and light.

Thy thousand thousand hosts are spread,
  Enbattled o'er the azure sky;

But Michael bears thy standard dread,
  And lifts the mighty cross on high.
He in that sign the rebel powers
  Did with their dragon prince expel ;
And hurled them from the heaven's high towers,
  Down like a thunderbolt to hell.
Grant us with Michael still, O Lord,
  Against the prince of pride to fight;
So may a crown be our reward,
  Before the Lamb's pure throne of light.
Now to the Father and the Son,
  Who rose from death, all glory be;
With thee, O holy Comforter,
  Henceforth through all eternity.

(Withim the Octave of the Ascension.)

Glory to Jesus, who returns
  In pomp triumphant to the sky,
With thee, O Father, and with thee,
  O holy Ghost eternally.

The Precious Blood.
(FROM THE ITALIAN).

HAIL, Jesus ! Hail ! who for my sake
Sweet Blood from Mary's veins didst take,
  And shed it all for me ;
O blessed be my Saviour's Blood,
My life, my light, my only good,
  To all eternity.

To endless ages let us praise
The Precious Blood whose price could raise
   The world from wrath and sin
Whose streams our inward thirst appease,
And heal the sinners worst disease,
   If he but bathe therein.

O sweetest Blood, that can implore
Pardon of God, and heaven restore,
   The heaven which sin hath lost :
While Abels's blood for vengeance pleade
What Jesus shed still intercedes
   For those wrong him most.

O to be sprinkled from the wells
Of Christ's own sacred Blood, excels
   Earth's best and highest bliss :
The ministers of wrath divine
Hurt not the happy hearts that shine
   With those red drops of His!

Ah! there is joy amid the Saints,
And hell's despairing courage faints
   When this sweet song we raise :
O louder then, and louder still,
Earth with one mighty chorus fill,
   The Precious Blood to praise!

   To all the faithful who say or sing the above Hymn. Pius VII, grants an indulgence of 100 days applicable also to the souls in Purgatory.

HYMNS. 401

" He hath ' given His Angels charge over thee to keep in all thy ways.'—Ps. xc.

To my Guardian Angel.

MORNING.

GUARDIAN Angel, thou hast kept
Watch around me while I slept :
Free from harm and peril now
With the Cross I sign my brow ;
Risen with the rising sun,
Forth I go, but not alone :
For, my keeper and my guide,
Thou art ever by my side,
Pour them ever in mine ear
Words which angels joy to hear ;
Curb thou my tongue and thoughts within
And keep my wandering eye from sin :
And rule my steps along the road
Which brings me nearer to my God.

Glory to the Father be,
Glory, Jesu Christ, to Thee,
And Holy Ghost, eternal Three.
Amen.

EVENING.

HOLY guardin Angel keep
Watch around me while I sleep ;
'Neath the shelter of thy wings
Save me from all hurtful things :

Pour the light, of love divine
In this cold dull heart of mine ;
Evil spirits drive away,
That I may rise at break of day
Again to praise my God and pray.

Glory to the Father be,
Glory Jesu Christ, to Thee.
And Holy Ghost, eternal Three.
Amen.

How much reverence ought this word to induce in thee; how much devotion bring along with it; how much confidence bestow! Reverence for the presence; devotion for the benevolence; confidence for the guardianship. In every inn, in every corner, reverence thine Angel. »— ST. BERNARD.

~~~~~

A Hymn for Little Children.
ON THE INFANCY OF JESUS.

Jesus, Thou wert meek and mild,
Thou wert once a little child ;—
Lo ! a little child to Thee
Saviour dear, I bend my knee ;
Make me gentle, mild, and meek,
Make me, Lord, Thy face to seek.

In a manger Thou wert born ;
Jesu, teach Thy child to scorn
This world's riches, and with Thee
Live content in poverty.

Once in Nazareth's humble cot
Thou didst taste of childhood's lot ;

And while summers rolled on
Thou wert rear'd as Joseph's son—
Son of the humble carpenter,
Torough of high heaven and earth the heir.
Pure Thou wert from taint of sin,
For the Godhead dwelt within.
Him thou didst obey, and Her,
Mary, Thine own Mother dear;
Blessed above women She!
Blessed above all in thee!
On thine infant face meanwhile,
Oft she shed a mothe'rs smile,
As she joyed to look upon
Thee her first and only Son.
Virgin Mother! ever blest,
Mary, teach me on thy breast
With thy Jesus there to rest.
Mother, keep me meek and mild,
Keep me with Him for thy child,
That, Jesus, I may live to Thee
In holy Christian infancy.

And as on each year doth flow,
Teach me still in grace to grow;
Teach me ever to obey,
Never from Thy steps to stray;
By They Cross and precious Blood,
Make me holy, chaste, and good
Bow my will, that when at last
Christian childhood shall be past,

I may love and serve Thee too,
And in heaven Thy sweetness know.
Glory to the Father be,
Glory Jesu Christ to Thee,
And Holy Ghost, Eternal Three !
Amen !

« From His earliest infancy, the blessed Jesus began to carry His cross, in order to teach us that no period of live is without its crosses. 'Follow Me, 'sait He; ' carry your cross after Me. ' Keep your eyes fixed on your divine pattern, and you will soon attain to the height of perfection, and, in the end, to everlasting felicity. » - NOUET.

∼∼∼∼

« *Suffer the Little Children to come unto Me* »

I think when I read that sweet story of old,
  When Jesus was here among men,
How he called little children, like lambs to his fold.
  I should like to have been with Him then.
How I wish that His hands had been laid on my head,
    And my arms had been thrown round His knee,
And that I might have seen His kind looks when He said.
  « Let the little ones come unto Me. »
Yet still to His foot stool in prayer I may go,
  And ask for a share of His love ;

And if I thus earnestly seek Him below,
    I shall see Him and hear Him above
In that beautiful place He has gone to prepare
    For all who are washed and forgiven,
For many dear children are gathering there,
    And « of such is the Kingdom of Heaven. »
Yet why should I think He's no longer on earth.
    When He says, « I am all days with you ? »
For sure, if He loves little children, like me,
    Then His words must be simple and true
No: He cannot deceive—His dear Mother I'll call,
    And straight to his altar repair ;
For they say he still dwells in that sweet holy
    place,
    And an infant may worship him there.

Home.

Oh ! how I love you, father dear !
    I love my mother too :
I've none in all this happy world
    One half so dear as you.
Sisters and brothers, each in turn,
    Share all my joys and fears ;
O ! what a bright glad home is mine !
    This home of smiles and tears.
But then, you tell me, I have got
    A dearer home above ;
A scene where sorrow enters not,
    A home of peace and love.

For worldly joys, though bright they shine
   Come quick, and then decay,
And parents'love, and eartly smiles
   Of home soon pass away.

What though I have a father here,
   That father has been given
To lead my infant heart to love
   « Our Father » dear « in Heaven. »

And mother's love, so fond, so pure,
   Oh! what is that to me,
As often as l Think upon
   The love that dwells in Thee.

Mary, dear Mother of my Lord,
   So « blest » so « full of grace ? »
Dear Mother of Christ's little ones ;
   Oh! how I love Thy face ?

Thus, all I see on this glad earth,
   Faint types and shadows are,
Of joys that fade not in the sky—
   That home so bright and fair.

Hymn of St. Francis Xavier.

O Deus, ego amo Te.

My God, I love Thee, not because
   I hope for heav'n thereby ;
Nor because they, who love Thee not,
   Must burn eternally.

Thou, O my Jesus, Thou didst me
 Upon the Cross embrace ;
For me didst bear the nails and spear,
 And manifold disgrace;

And griefs and torments numberless;
 And sweat of agony;
E'en death itself—and all for one
 Who was Thine enemy.

Then why, O blessed Jesus Christ!
 Should I not love Thee well ;
Not for the sake of winning heaven,
 Or of escaping hell :

Not with the hope af gaining aught
 Not seeking a reward ;
But, as Thyself hast loved me,
 O ever-loving Lord ?

E'en so I love thee, and will love,
 And in Thy praise will sing;
Solely because Thou art my God,
 And my eternal King

The Lord possessed me in the beginning of his ways, before he made any thing from the beginning. I was ordained from eternity, and of old before the earth was made. The depths were not as yet, and I was already conceived.

The Immaculate Conception.

O PUREST of creatures ! sweet Mother ! sweet Maid !
Thee one spotless womb wherein Jesus was laid !
Dark night hath come down on us, Mother ! and we
Look out for thy shining, sweet Star of the Sea!

Deep night hath come down on this rough-spoken world,
And the banners of darkness are boldly unfurled ;
And the tempest-tost Ghurch-all her eyes are on thee,
They look to thy shining, sweet Star of the Sea !

The Church doth what God had first taught her to do ;
He looked o'er the world to find hearts that were true :
Through the ages He looked, and He found none but thee,
And he loved thy clear shining, sweet Star of the Sea !

He gazed on thy soul ; it was spotless and fair ;
For the empire of sin—it had never been there.
None had e'er owned thee, dear Mother ! but He,
And He blessed thy clear shinning, sweet Star of the Sea !

Earth gave Him one lodging ; 'twas deep in thy breast,
And God found a home where the sinner finds rest ;
His home ad His hiding-place, both were in thee,
He was won by thy shining, sweet Star of the Sea !

O blissful and calm was the wonderful rest
That thou gavest thy God in thy virginal breast;
For the Heaven He left He found Heaven in thee,
And He shone in thy shining, sweet Star of the Sea !

To sinners what comfort, to angels what mirth,
That God found one creature unfallen on earth,
One spot where His Spirit untroubled could be,
The depths of thy shining, sweet Star of the Sea !

So age after age in the Church had gone round,
And the Saints new inventions of homage have found,
New titles of honor, new honors for thee,
New love for thy shining, sweet Star of the Sea !

And now from the Church of all lands thy dear name
Comes borne on the breath of one migthy acclaim ;
Men call on their father, that He should decree
A new gem to thy shining, sweet Star of the Sea !

O shine on us brigther than ever, then, shine !
For the primest of honors, dear Mother! is thine;
« Conceived without sin, « thy new title shall
 be,
Clear light from thy birth-spring, sweet Star of
 the Sea !

So worship we God in these rude latter days ;
So worship we Jesus our love, when we
 praise
His wonderful grace in the gifts He gave
 thee,
The gift of clear shining, sweet Star of the
 Sea !

Deep night hath come down on us, Mother
 deep night.
And we need more than ever the guide of thy
 light ;
For the darker the night is, the brighter should
 be
Thy beautiful shining, sweet Star of the Sea !

O God, who, by the immaculate Conception of
the Virgin, didst prepare for thy Son an habitation
worthy of him ; grant us, by her intercession,
faithfully to keep our hearts and bodies immaculate
for thee, who didst preserve her from all stain.
Through the same our Lord &c. Amen.

I am a Faithful Catholic.

I am a faithful Catholic,
   I love my Holy Faith,
I will be true to Holy Church,
   And steadfast unto death.

I shun the haunts of those who seek
   To ensnare poor Catholic youth ;
No Church I own, no Schools I know,
   Buth those that teach the Thruth.

If base it is to yield before
   The Persecutor's Rod ;
Then baser far to side with those,
   Who insult the Church of God.

Oh ! far from me such wickedness !
   One treasure I hold dear,
MY HOLY FAITH. I fear not men,
   'Tis God alone I fear.

I love His Altar, where I kneel
   My Jesus to adore ;
I love my Mother Mary dear,
   Oh ! may I love them more.

I love the Saints of olden time,
   The places where they dwelt ;
I love to pray where Saints have prayed,
   And kneel where they have knelt.

I love my Cross, I love my Beads—
Each Emblem of my Faith ;
Let foolish men rail as they will,
I'll love them until death.

Two Thousand Years Ago

Two thousand years, two thousand years,
  Our bark, o'er billowy seas,
Has onward kept her steady course
  Through hurricane and breeze.
Her Captain was the Risen One—
  She braved the stormy foe :
And still He guides, who guided her
  Two thousand years ago ;
And still He guides, who guided her
  Two thousand years ago.

When first our gallant ship was launch'd,
  Altho' our hands were few,
Yet dauntless was each bosom found,
  And every heart was true !
And still though in her mighty hull,
  Unnumber'd bosom's glow ;
Her crew is faithful as it was
  Two thousand years ago ;
Her crew is faithful as it was
  Two thousand years ago.

True, some had left this noble craft,
   To sail the seas alone,
And made them in their hour of pride
   A vessel of their own;
But when portentous clouds did rise,
   Tempestous storms did blow,
They re-entered that old vessel built
   Two thousand years ago.

For onward rides our gallant bark,
   With all her canvas set,
In some few nations stil unknown,
   To plant her standard yet—
Her flag shall float where e'er a breath
   From human life shall glow;
And millions bless the bark that sail'd
   Two thousand years ago!
And millions bless the bark that sail'd
   Two tousand years ago!

True to that guiding star which led
   To Israels cradled hope,
Her steady needle pointeth yet
   To Calvary's bloody top!
Yes! there she floats, that good old ship,
   From mast to keel below,
Sweaworthy still, as erst she was,
   Two thousand years ago!
Seaworthy still, as erst she was,
   Two thousand years ago

Not unto us—not unto us—
   Be praise or glory given,
But unto him who watch and ward
   Hath kept for her in Heaven.
Who quelled the whirlwind in its wrath,
   Bade tempests cease to blow,
The Lord, who launch'd our vessel forth,
   Two thousand years ago!
The Lord, who launch'd our vessel forth,
   Two thousand years ago!

Then onward speed thee, brave old bark,
   Speed onward in thy pride,
O'er sunny seas and billows dark,
   The Holy One thy guide:
And sacred be each plank and spar,
   Unchang'd by friend or foe,
Just as she left Jerusalem—
   Two thousand years ago!
Just as she left Jerusalem—
   Two thousand years ago!

Daily, Daily, Sing to Mary.

Daily, daily, sing to Mary,
   Sing, my soul, her praises due,
All her feasts, her actions worship,
   With the heart's devotion true.
Lost in wond'ring contemplation,
   Be her majesty confest;
Call her Mother, call her Virgin,
Happy Mother, Virgin blest.

She is mighty do deliver,
   Call her, trust her lovingly,
When the tempest rages round thee
   She will calm the troubled sea.
Gifts of heaven she has given,
   Noble Lady! to our race:
She the Queen, who decks her subjects
   With the light of God's own grace.

Sing my tongue the Virgin's trophies,
   Who for us her Maker bore;
For the curse of old inflicted
   Peace and blessing to restore.
Sing in songs of praise unending,
   Sing the world's majestic Queen;
Weary not nor faint in telling
   All the gifts she gives to men.

All my senses, heart, affections,
   Strive to sound her glory forth;
Spread abroad the sweet memorials
   Of the Virgin's priceless worth.
Where the voice of music thrilling?
   Where the tongue of eloquence,
That can utter hymns beseeming
   All her matchless excellence?

All our joys do flow from Mary,
   All then join her praise to sing;
Trembling sing the Virgin Mother,
   Mother of our Lord and King.

While we sing her awful glory,
　Far above our fancy's reach;
Let our hearts be quick to offer
　Love the heart alone can teach.

Sweet Month of May.

Joy of our hearts! O let us pay
　To thee tine own sweet month of May;
Mary one gif we beg of thee—
　Our souls from sin and sorrow free;
　Our souls from sin and sorrow free.
Direct our wand'ring feet aright,
　And be thyself our own true light,
Be love of theé the purging fire,
　To cleanse for God our heart's desire:
　To cleanse for God our heart's desire.
Joy of our hearts! O let us pay
　To thee thine own sweet month of May.

Mother of God, to us no les,
　Vouchsafe a Mother's sweet caress;
Oh, Jesus, Mary, Joseph, deign
　Our souls in heavenly ways to train;
　Our souls in heavenly ways to train.
Dear Mother be love of thee a ray,
　From heav'n to show the heav'nward way.
Be love of thee our whole life long,
　A seal upon our wayward tongue,
　A seal upon our wayward tongue.
Joy of our hearts! O let us pay,
　To thee thine own sweet month of May.

Thou who wert pure as driven snow,
    Make us as thou wert here below,
Oh, queen of Heaven? obtain that we
    Thy glory there one day may see;
    Thy glory there one day may see;
Write on our frail heart's deepest core,
    The five dear wounds that Jesus bore,
And give us tears to shed with thee,
    Beneath the Cross ou Calvary,
    Beneath the Cross on Calvary.
Joy of our hearts! O let us pay,
    To thee thine own sweet month of May.
When mute before the Judge we stand,
    Our holy shield be Mary's hand;
Oh, Mother let no child of thine
    In hell's eternal exile pine;
    In hell's eternal exile pine.
One more request and we have done
    With love of thee and thy dear Son.
More let us burn, and more each day,
    Till love of self is burn'd away,
    Till love of self is burn'd away.
Joy of our hearts! O let us pay,
    To thee thine own sweet month of May.

I am a Little Catholic.

I am a little Catholic,
   And Christian is my name,
And I believe the Holy Church
   In ev'ry age the same.

I love her Altars where I kneel
   My Jesus to adore;
I love my Mother, Mary dear.
   Oh, may I love them more.

I love the Saints of olden time,
   The places where they dwelt;
I love to pray where Saints have pray'd.
   And kneel where they have knelt.

I love the Holy Sacraments,
   They bring me near to God;
The Church points out the way to Heav'n.
   These help me on the road.

I love the priests, my pastors dear,
   They have left all for me;
Next to my parents here on earth,
   I love them tenderly.

I am a little Catholic,
   I love my Holy Faith;
I will be true to Holy Church,
   And steadfast until death.

HYMNS.

St. Patrick.

Hail, glorious S Patrick, dear saint of our isle!
On us, thy poor children, bestow a smeet
  smile;
And now thou art high in thy mansions above,
On Erin's green valleys look down in thy
  love.
On Erin's green valleys look down in thy
  love.

Hail, glorious St. Patrick, thy words were once
  strong,
Against satan's wiles and a heretic throng:
Not less in thy might where in heaven thou
  art;
Oh, come to our, aid, in our battle take
  part.
Oh, come to our aid, in our battle take part.

In the war against sin, in the fight for the
  faith,
Dear saint, may thy children resist to the
  death,
May their strength be in meekness, in penance,
  in prayer,
Their banner the cross which they glory to
  bear,
Their banner the cross which they glory to
  bear.

Thy people, now exiles on many a shore,
Shall love and revere thee till time be no
    more;
And the fire thou hast kindled shall ever
    burn bright,
Its warmth undiminished, undying its light,
Its warmth undiminished, undying its light.

Ever bless and defend the sweet land of our
    birth,
Where the shamrock stil blooms as when thou
    wert on earth;
And our hearts shall yet burn where-so-ever we
    roam,
For God and St. Patrick, and our native
    home.
For God and St. Patrick, and our native
    home.

All praise to St. Patrick.

All praise to St. Patrick, who brought to our
    mountains
  The gift of God's faith, the sweet light of his
    love!
All praise to the shepherd who show'd us the
    fountains
  That rise in the Heart of the Saviour
    above!

For hundreds of years,
In smiles and in tears,
Our Saint hath been with us, our shield and
  our stay;
All else may have gone;
St. Patrick alone,
He hath been to us light when earth's lights
  were all set,
For the glories of faith they can never decay;
And the best of our glories is bright with us
  yet.
In the faith and the feast of St. Patrick's
  Day.

There is not a saint in the bright courts of
  heaven
More faithful than he to the land of his
  choice;
Oh, well may the nation to whom he was
  given;
In the feast of their sire and apostle rejoice!
In glory above,
True to his love,
He keeps the false faith from his children
  away;
The dark false faith,
Far worse than death,
O he drives it far off from the green sunny
  shore,
Like the reptiles which fled from his curse
  in dismay;

And Erin, when error's proud triumph is o'er,
  Will still be found keeping St. Patrick's Day.
Then what shall we do for thee, heaven sent
    father?
  What shall the proof of our loyalty be?
By all that is dear to our hearts, we would
    rather
  Be martyr'd, sweet Saint! than bring shame
    upon thee!
      But oh! he will take
      The promise we make
So to live that our lives by God's help may
    display
      The light that he bore
      To Erin's shore—
Yes! Father of Ireland, no child wilt thou own,
  Whose life is not lighted by grace on its way;
For they are true Irish. O yes, they alone,
  Whose hearts are all true on St. Patrick's Day.

The Month of Mary.

Snow and rain have vanished,
  Winds have ceased to wail,
Gloomy winter's banished
  From the hill and dale.

CHORUS.—Gentle Mother hear us,
  At thy altar pray,
Queen of Saints, be near us
  On this sweet May-day.

Spring hath come with flowers,
  Spring hath come with light,
Soft and rosy hours
  Fill the day and night.
    CHORUS—Gentle Mother, etc.

Stars above us gleaming,
  Tell of Mary's worth,
Blossoms 'round us teeming,
  Speak her praise to earth.—CHORUS.

Here below deserving
  She was found alone,
God from sin preserving,
  Chose her for his own.—CHORUS.

Grace as to none other,
  Grace to her was given,
She became the mother,
  Of the King of heaven.— CHORUS.

God bestowed upon her
  Glories all her own,
Earth's sublimest honor,
  Heaven's queenly throne.—CHORUS.

Taught by Him wo love her,
  In our simply way,
Placing none above her,
  On this sweet May-day.—CHORUS.

God Bless Our Pope.

Full in the panting heart of Rome,
  Beneath the Apostle's crowning dome,

HYMNS.

From pilgrims lips that kiss the ground
  Breathes in all tongues one only sound :
  « God bless our Pope, the great, the good. »
  « God bless our Pope, the great, the good. »

The golden roof, the marble walls,
  The Vatican's majestic halls,
The note redouble ; till it fills
  With echoes sweet the seven hills ;
  « God bless our Pope, the great, the good. »
  « God bless our Pope, the great, the good. »

Then surging through each hallowed gate,
  Where martyrs glory en peace await,
It sweeps beyond the solemn plain,
  Peals over Alps across the main :
  « God bless our Pope, the great, the good. »
  « God bless our Pope, the great, the good. »

From torrid south to frozen north,
  The wave harmonious stretches forth,
Yet strikes no chord more true to Rome's
  That rings within our hearts and homes :
  « God bless our Pope, the great, the good. »
  « God bless our Pope, the great, the good. »

For like the sparks of unseen fire,
  That speak along the magic wire,
From home to home, heart to heart,
  These words of countless children dart :
  « God bless our Pope, the great, the good. »
  « God bless our Pope, the great, the good. »

Te Deum laudámus : * Te Dóminum confitémur.

Te ætérnem Patrem * omnis terra venerátur.

Tibi omnes angeli, * tibi cœli, et univérsæ potestátes :

Tibi chérubim et séraphim, * incessábili voce proclámant :

Sanctus, sanctus, sanctus, * Dóminus Deus Sábaoth :

Pleni sunt cœli et terra, * majestátis glóriæ tuæ.

Te gloriósus * Apostolórum chorus.

Te Prophetárum * laudábilis númerus.

Te Mártyrum candidátus * laudat exércitus.

Te per orbem terrárum * sancta confité-

We praise thee, O God : we acknowledge thee to be the Lord.

All the earth doth worship thee ; the Father everlasting.

To thee all angels cry aloud; the heavens and all the powers therein :

To thee cherubim and seraphim : continually do cry :

Holy, holy, holy : Lord God of Sabaoth.

Heaven and earth are full of the majesty of thy glory.

The glorious choir of the Apostles : praise thee.

The admirable company of the Prophets : praise thee.

The white-robed army of Martyrs : praise thee.

The Holy Church throughout all the

tur Ecclésia.

Patrem * imménsæ majestátis.

Venerándum tuum verum * et unicum Fílium.

Sanctum quoque * Paráclitum Spíritum.

Tu Rex glóriæ, * Christe.

Tu Patris * sempitérnus es Fílius.

Tu ad liberándum susceptúrus hóminem, * non horruísti Vírginis úterum.

Tu devicto mortis acúleo, * ab eruísti credéntibus regna cœlórum.

Tu ad déxteram Dei sedes, * in glória Patris.

Judex créderis * esse ventúrus.

* Te ergo quæsumus tuis fámulis súbveni, * quos pretióso sánguine

world ; doth acknowledge thee.

The Father : of an infinite majesty.

Thy adorable true : and only Son.

Also the Holy Ghost : the Comforter.

Thou art the King of Glory : O Christ.

Thou art the everlasting Son : of the Father.

When thou lookest upon thee of deliver man : thou didst not abhor the virgin's womb.

When thou hadst overcome the sting of death : thou didst open the kingdom of heaven to all believers.

Thou sittest at the right hand of God : in the glory of the Father.

We believe that thou shalt come : to be our Judge.

We pray thee, therefore, help thy servants : whom thou hast

TE DEUM LAUDAMUS.

redemisti.

Ætérna fac cum Sanctis tuis, * in glória numerári.

Salvum fac pópulum tuum, Domine, * et bénedic hæreditáti tuæ.

Et rege eos, et extólle illos, * usque in ætérnum.

Per singulos dies * benedícimus te.

Et laudámus nomen tuum in sæculum, * et in sæculum sæculi.

Dignáre, Dómine, die isto, * sine peccáta nos custodíre.

Miserére nostri, Dómine, * miserére nostri.

Fiat miséricordia tua Dómine, super nos * quemádmodum sperávimus in te.

In te, Dómine, sperávi; * non confundar in æternum.

redeemed with thy precious blood.

Make them to be numbered with thy Saints : in glory everlasting.

O Lord, save thy people : and bless thine inheritance.

Govern them : and lift them up for ever.

Day by day : we magnify thee.

And we praise thy name for ever : yea, for ever and ever.

Vouchsafe, O Lord, this day : to keep us without sin.

O Lord, have mercy upon us : have mercy upon us.

O Lord, let thy mercy be showed upon us : as we have hoped in thee.

O Lord, in thee have I hoped : let me not be confounded for ever.

V. Benedicamus Patrem et Filium, cum Sancto Spiritu.

R. Laudemus et super exaltemus eum in sæcula.

Oremus.

Deus, cujus misericordiæ non est numerus, et bonitatis infinitus est thesaurus piissimæ majestati tuæ pro collatis donis gratias agimus, tuam semper clementiam exorantes: ut qui petentibus postulata concedis, eosdem non deserens, ad præmia futura disponas.

R. Amen.

V. Let us bless the Father and the Son, with the Holy Ghost.

R. Let us praise and magnify him for ever.

Let us Pray.

O God, whose mercies are without number, and the treasure of whose goodness is infinite; we render thanks to thy most gracious Majesty for the gifts thou hast bestowed upon us, evermore beseeching thy clemency: that as thou grantest the petitions of them that ask thee, thou wilt never forsake them, but wilt prepare them for the rewards to come.

ASPERGES;

OR,

SPRINKLING OF THE HOLY WATER.

Before solemn Mass, From Trinity *to* Palm Sunday *inclusively, the following* Anthem *is sung :*

Ant. ASPERGES me, Domine, hysopo, et nundabor ; lavabis me, et super nivem dealbabor.

Ps. Miserere mei, Deus, secundum magnam misericordiam tuam.
V. Gloria, etc.
Ant. Asperges, me, &c.

Ant. SPRINKLE me, with hyssop O Lord, and I shall be cleansed ; wash me and I shall be whiter than snow.

Ps. Have mercy on me, O God, according to thy great mercy.
V. Glory, &c.
Ant. Sprinkle me, etc.

The Priest being returned to the food of the Altar, says :

V. Ostende nobis, Domine, misericordiam tuam.

V. Show us, O Lord, thy mercy.

R. Et salutare tuum da nobis.

V. Domine, exaudi orationem meam.

R. Et clamor meus ad te veniat.

V. Dominis vobiscum.

R. Et cum spiritu tuo.

R. And grant us thy salvation.

V. O Lord, hear my prayer.

R. And let my cry come unto thee.

V. The Lord be with you.

R. And with thy spirit.

Let us Pray.

Exaudi nos, Domine Sancte, Pater omnipotens, æterne Deus : et mittere digneris sanctum angelum tuum de cœlis, qui custodiat, faveat, protegat, visitet, atque defendat omnes habitantes in hoc habitaculo, per Christum Dominum nostrum. *Amen.*

Hear us, O holy Lord, Almighty Father, eternal God, and vouchsafe to send thy angel from heaven to guard, cherish, protect, visit, and defend all that are assembled in this place ; through Jesus Christ our Lord. *Amen.*

ANTHEMS.

From Easter *to* Whitsunday *inclusively, the following is sung:*

VIDI aquam egredientem de templo à latere dextro, *Alleluia*; et omnes ad quos pervenit aqua ista, salvi facti sunt, et discent, *Alleluia.*

I SAW water flowing from the right side of the temple, *Alleluia*; and all to whom that water came were saved, and they shall say, *Alleluia.*

Ps. Confitemini Domino, quoniam bonus; quoniam in sæculum misericordia ejus. Gloria, &c.

Ps. Praise the Lord, because he is good; because his mercy endureth for ever. Glory, &c.

A PRAYER FOR THE AUTHORITIES.

WE pray Thee, O Almighty and Eternal God, Who, trough Jesus Christ, hast revealed Thy glory to all nations, to preserve the works of Thy mercy; that Thy Church, being spread trough the whole world, may continue with un changing faith, in the confession of Thy name.

We pray Thee. Who alone art good and holy, to endow with heavenly knowledge, sincere zeal, and sauctity of live, our chief Bishop *(name him,)* the Vicar of our Lord Jesus Christ, in the government of His Church ; our own Bishop, *(name him,)* all other Bishops, Prelates and Pastors of the Church, and especially those who are appointed to exercise amongst us the functions of the holy ministry, and conduct Thy people into the ways of salvation.

We pray Thee, O God of might, wisdom, and justice, through whom authority is rightly administered, laws are enacted, and judgment decreed, assist, with Thy Holy Spirit of counsel and fortitude, the President of these United States ; that his administration may be conducted in righteousness, and be eminently useful to Thy people over whom he presides, by encouraging due respect for virtue and religion ; by a faithful execution of the laws in justice and mercy ; and by restraining vice and immorality. Let the light of Thy Divine wisdom direct the deliberations of Congress, and shine forth in all their proceedings, and laws enacted for our rule and government; so that they may tend to the preservation of peace, the promotion of national happiness, the increase of industry, sobriety, and useful knowledge, and may perpetuate to us the blessings of equal liberty.

We pray for his Excellency, the Governor of this state, for the Members of Assembly, for all Judges, Magistrates, and other Officers, who are appointed to guard our political welfare ; that they may be enabled by thy powerful protection, to discharge the duties of their respective stations with honesty and ability.

We recommend, likewise, to Thy unbounded mercy, all our brethren and fellow-citizens, throughout the United States, that they may be blessed in the knowledge, and sanctified in the observance of Thy most holy Law; that they may be preserved in union, and in that peace which the world cannot give; and after enjoying the blessings of this life, be admitted to those which are eternal.

Finally, we pray Thee, O Lord of mercy to remember the souls of Thy servants departed, who are gone before us, with the sign of faith, and repose in the sleep of peace; the souls of our parents, relations, and friends; of those, who, when living, were members of this congregation; and particulary of such as are lately deceased; of all benefactors, who, by their donations or legacies to this church, witnessed their zeal for the decency of divine worship, and proved their claim to our grateful and charitable remembrance. To these, O Lord, and to all that rest in Christ, grant, we beseech Thee, a place of refreshment, light, and everlasting peace : Through the same Jesus Christ our Lord and Saviour. Amen.

THE MANNER OF
Serving and Answering at Mass.

When the persons or acolytes who are to serve at Mass go from the sacristy, they proceed before the priest, and stand back for him to pass, kneel making a reverence whilst the priest ascends to place the chalice on the altar; when several persons attend the priest they must do as near as possible as the one who serves him, and where the blessed Sacrament is kept, all who enter the oratory or chancel must make a reverence.

When the priest returns to the foot of the altar, and placing himself between the acolytes and bowing down before it, he signs himself with the sign of the ✠ from the forehead to the breast, and says with a distinct voice as follows, which the assistants answer.

PRIEST. ✠ In nomine Patris, et Filii, et Spiritus Sancti.

CLERK. *Amen.*

P. Introibo ad altare Dei.

C. Ad Deum, qui lætificat juventutem meam.

P. Judica me, Deus, et discerne causam meam de gente non sancta ; ab homino iniquo et doloso erue me.

C. Quia tu es, Deus, fortitudo, mea: quare me repulisti, et quare tristis incedo dum affligit me inimicus.

P. Emitte lucem tuam et veritatem tuam : ipsa me deduxerunt, et adduxerunt in montem sanctum tuum, et in tabernacula tua.

C. Et introibo ad altare Dei: ad Deum, qui lætificat juventutem meam.

P. Confitebor tibi in cithara, Deus, Deus meus : quare tristis es, anima mea, et quare conturbas me ?

C. Spera in Deo, quoiniam adhuc confitebor illi : salutare vultus mei, et Deus meus.

P. Gloria Patri, et Filio, et spiritui Sancto.

C. Sicut erat in principio, et nunc, et semper, et in sæcula sæculorum. — *Amen.*

P. Introibo ad altare Dei.

C. Ad Deum, qui lætificat juventutem meam.

SERVING AT MASS. 437

P. Adjutorium nostrum in nomine Domini.
C. Qui fecit cœlum et terram.
P. Confiteor Deo, &c.

When the Priest begins the Confiteor bow your head until you have finished it.

C. Miseratur tui, omnipotens Deus : et dimissis peccatis tuis, perducat te ad vitam æternam. P. *Amen.*

C. Confiteor Deo omnipotenti, beatæ Mariæ semper Virgini, beato Michaeli archangelo, beato Joanni Baptistæ, sanctis Apostolis Petro et Paulo, omnibus sanctis, et tibi Pater : (*turn your head towards the Priest and say,*) quia peccavi nimis cogitatione, verbo, et opere ; (*strike your breast three times, saying,*) meâ culpâ, meâ culpâ meâ maximâ culpâ. Ideo precor beatam Mariam semper Virginem, beatum Michaelem Archangelum, beatum Joannem Baptistam, sanctos apostolos Petrum et Paulum, omnes Sanctos, et te Pater, (*turn towards the Priest*), orare pro me ad Dominum Deum nostrum.

P. Misereatur vestri, &c.
C. *Amen.*
P. Indulgentiam, absolutionem, &c.
C. *Amen.*
P. Deus, tu conversus vivificabis nos.
C. Et plebs tua lætabitur in te.
P. Ostende nobis, Domine misericordiam tuam.
C. Et salutare tuum da nobis.
P. Domine, exaudi orationem meam.
C. Et clamor meus ad te veniat.
P. Dominus vobiscum.
C. Et cum spiritu tuo.

Then rise and kneel on the lower step of the altar.
When the priest is going up to the altar, hold up his alb or cassock.
[At grand and solemn Masses, the high priest is here served by the deacon with the cencer, the sub-deacon holds the book of the altar while he incenses it, then the deacon receiving it from the priest incenses him.]

P. Kyrie eleison.
C. Kyrie eleison.
P. Kyrie eleison.
C. Christe eleison.

P. Christe eleison.
C. Christe eleison.
P. Kyrie eleison.
C. Kyrie eleison.
P. Kyrie eleison.
P. Dominus vobiscum, *or* Flectamus genua.
C. Et cum spiritu tuo, *or* Levate.
P. Per omnia sæcula sæculorum.
C. *Amen.*

At the end of the Epistle say,

Deo gratias.

The gradual tract or *Alleluia* being read remove the Mass book to the Gospel side ; making reverence as you pass before the middle of the altar ; after which return and stand at the Epistle side.

P. Dominus vobiscum.
C. Et cum spiritu tuo.
P. Sequentia sancti Evangelii secundum, &c.

Make the sign of the ✝ first on your forehead ; second, on your mouth ; third, on your breast ; and say :

Gloria tibi Domino.

« At grant and solemn Masses, the censer is here given to the priest, who incenses the book, and also after the Gospel to the deacon to incense the Priest ; if there be no deacon or sub-deacon, the assistant does it himself. »]

Make a reverence at the beginning and end of the Gospel, at the name of Jesus, and at the end say :

C. Laus tibi, Christe.

At the words, ET INCARNATUS ET SPIRITU SANCTI in the creed, kneel and make a reverence.

[At High Mass, while the choir sings the credo, and the clergy pause until its conclusion, light the elevation candles, if any.]

P. Dominus vobiscum.
C. Et cum spiritu tuo.

Go to the middle of Altar, make a reverence, then proceed to the credence-table, prepare the wine and water, taking the wine tn the right, and the water in the left hand ; give the wine with your right hand and receive it with your left, that you may present the water with your right, make a reverence to the Priest before and after ; put the towel neatly folded on the end of the Altar, then hold the cruet in your right and the

SERVING AT MASS. 441

plate with your left hand, pour water on the fingers of the priest ; after placing the cruets in their former position, and having received the towel, place it on the table ; return after making a reverence in the middle, and kneel at the Epistle side of the Altar.

At Grand and Solemn Masses, the Priest is here served with the censer the same as at first and the deacon receiving the censer from the Priest, incenses him, then the choir, and sub-deacon ; after which, the sub deacon receiving it, incenses the deacon, the acolytes, and lastly, the congregation.]

P. Orate, Fratres, &c.

C. Suscipiat Dominus sacrificium de manibus tuis ad laudem et gloriam nominis sui, ad utilitatem quoque nostram, totiusque ecclesiæ suæ sanctæ.

P. Per omnia sæcula sæculorum.

C. *Amen.*

P. Dominus vobiscum.

C. Et cum spiritu tuo.

P. Sursum corda.

C. Habemus ad Dominum.

P. Gratias agamus Domino Deo nostro.

C. Dignum et justum est.

At *Sanctus, Sanctus, Sanctus*, &c., ring the bell, where this is customary. And again, when you see the Priest spread his hands over the chalice, give warning by the bell of the consecration which is about to be made. Then holding up the vestment with your left hand, and having the bell in your right, ring during the elevation of the Host; which being ended, you must kiss the vestment; and presently do the same at the elevation of the chalice. As often as you pass by the Blessed Sacrament, you must adore on your kness.

P. Per omnia sæcula sæculorum.
C. *Amen*.
P. Et ne nos inducas in tentationem.
C. Sed libera nos a malo.
P. Per omnia sæcula sæculorum.
C. *Amen*.
P. Pax Domini sit semper vobiscum.
C. Et cum spiritu tuo.

While the Priest striking his breast, says: *Domine non sum dignus*, ring the bell each time he pronounces those words. The Priest communion being ended, and when you see that he has received the chalice, it there be any communicants give them the cloth then returning kneel at the Epistle end of the Altar, say the *Confiteor*, ring the bell each time the Priest says, *Domine non sum dignus*; after the Blessed Sacrament is put in the tabernacle, make reverence at the centre of the Altar. Go to the credence-table, taking the wine in your right, and the water in your left, serve him with wine only, then retire a little back, pour first the wine, then the water, over the Priest's fingers, till he makes a motion for you to stop ; then put the cruets in their former place, go to the centre of the Altar and make a reverence ; remove the book from the Gospel to the Epistle side, and then retire to the Gospel side ; each time you pass the middle of the Altar knee, and make a reverence.

P. Dominus vobiscum.
C. Et cum spiritu tuo.
P. Ite, Missa est ; *or* Benedicamus Domino.
C. Deo gratias.

In Masses for the Dead.

P. Requiescant in pace.
C. *Amen.*

Remove the book if left open, to the Gospel side ; kneel in the centre, and receive the Priest's blessing.

P. Pater, et Filius, et Spiritus Sanctus.

C. *Amen.*

Then Rise, and at the beginning of the Gospel make the sign of the † on your forehead, mouth, and breast, and say :

P. Dominus vobiscum.
C. Et cum spiritu tuo.
P. Initium, *or* Sequentia Sancti Evangelii, &c.
C. Gloria tibi, Domine.

At the end of the Gospel, say, DEO GRATIAS.

www.ingramcontent.com/pod-product-compliance
Lightning Source LLC
Chambersburg PA
CBHW051722300426
44115CB00007B/428